POWER

FROM

Within

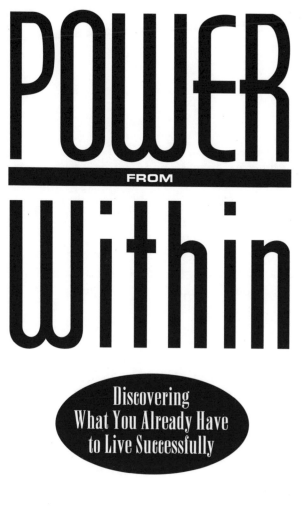

**Discovering
What You Already Have
to Live Successfully**

Danita Johnson Hughes

Power From Within
Discovering What You Already Have to Live Successfully

By Danita Johnson Hughes

Printed in the United States of America

Cover design and layout by Ad Graphics, Inc., Tulsa, Oklahoma

ISBN: 0-9706700-0-1

DEDICATION

✦

Dedicated to Lea and Ray. I believe in you.
Live your dreams. Find your purpose. The gifts you have
are uniquely yours. Open them and experience
their splendor.

ACKNOWLEDGMENTS

My heartfelt thanks go out to all the many people who have encouraged me to write this book. Somehow, they think that I have something to share that could possibly enhance the lives of others.

To my husband Chuck who took time to read and comment on certain chapters between football and/or basketball games, I owe a tremendous debt of gratitude. I am constantly amazed at how he could read and make intelligent comments on portions of the book while simultaneously concentrating on two different games, on different channels and never missing a play.

Thanks to my daughter Kyla who frequently put aside her homework to help me select meaningful quotes and who never missed a chance to infuse her thoughts on how to make the book better. She also took advantage of opportunities to correct her mother's grammar and to comment on her composition skills. At least I know the money for her education has been well spent.

Finally, thanks to my very dedicated team at Edgewater Systems for Balanced Living, the organization where I currently serve as president and chief executive officer. Their hard work and diversity of ideas and opinions are a constant source of inspiration. Many of them were very helpful in assisting me to come up with a title for this book. A special thanks goes out to Anthony Briscoe for suggesting the winning title.

TABLE OF CONTENTS

FOREWORD

❧

I've been an elementary school teacher all of my adult life and prepared myself to make a difference in the lives of my students. I've taught so many young people with potential and often wondered if they ever reached it. Teachers attempt to inspire their students to develop their learning skills to the fullest and to become successful, productive citizens.

When I learned of the accomplishments of Danita Johnson Hughes, I became elated and proud of her success. She built a positive self-image in the midst of possible discouragements. In her book, she does not avoid difficult social issues of poverty, abuse, and neglect. She emphasizes her need to build a positive attitude toward her education, interpersonal relations, and setting and successfully attaining goals in her life. The joys, the sorrows, the pain, the love, the hope, and the desire to achieve are bound together in this beautifully written book.

I am grateful that I had the opportunity to play a small role in her childhood. Thanks for remembering me and that classroom at Douglass Elementary School.

To Danita and all the students I have ever taught, it was through you that I remain eternally young at heart.

Gussie L. Kaufman

INTRODUCTION

❧

Talents, small or large, are God-given. They are a sacred trust.
                                                    – Paul Robeson

I hope this book does some good.

My desire is that it should be of benefit to others. I would want readers to profit from the experiences and thoughts I have put down on paper. I wrote it, not as a form of catharsis or an exercise in ego, but rather as a means of offering the lessons I have learned as lessons others may learn as well.

Benefiting others, trying to do some good in this troubled world of ours, has become so very central to my being.

It is, by and large, what I am all about.

It is, by and large, what we should all be about.

That wasn't always the case with me. There was a time when just getting by was the best I could hope to accomplish, and there were times when I didn't always manage that very well.

But I learned lessons from those times, and I am still learning.

In writing this book, I have not set out to make any claims that mine is or has been an extraordinary life.

True, there have been achievements, and there have been obstacles overcome in reaching them.

But others have achieved more and overcome even bigger obstacles.

I don't hold myself up as a shining example of success, but I do know this: Others who started out with far more advantages than I, have achieved a great deal less.

In the pages that follow, I have tried to record the influences that helped me rise above humble beginnings, the decisions that aided me in avoiding some mistakes and overcoming others, the factors that enabled me to get to a point in my life where I am happy and successful.

Quickly about me: I am sometimes referred to as a "Gary Girl," because I was born, reared and educated in Gary, Indiana, a city in which I continue to work and live. I attended public school in Gary and even went to college at a local branch of Indiana University, where I earned both bachelor's and master's degrees in public administration.

I also have a master's degree from the University of Chicago where I also received a graduate certificate in health administration and policy. I am currently a candidate for my doctorate at Walden University.

My life and career path have led me to my current position as president and chief executive officer of Edgewater Systems for Balanced Living, formerly known as the Gary Community Mental Health Center.

The abiding interest in the welfare of families, in human dynamics and in social service systems grew out of my own somewhat troubled childhood.

I've been there and now I'm here.

I like to think an examination of the steps I took along the way might assist others in getting from there to here.

That might do some good.

CHAPTER ONE

New Shoes and Shiny Dimes

❧

Each of us can look back upon someone who made a great difference in our lives, often a teacher whose wisdom or simple acts of caring made an impression upon us at a formative time. In all likelihood, it was someone who sought no recognition for their deed, other than the joy of knowing that, by their hand, another life had been made better.

– Stephen M. Wolf

Thank you, Mrs. Kaufman.

People help us in our lives practically every day. They do so in ways big and small. There are people who help us at every stage and in every phase of our lives. We should all take the time to thank them for this.

For me, it was a first grade teacher in my hometown of Gary, Indiana.

Thank you, Mrs. Kaufman.

She took the time and put forth the effort to make me feel special, when I wasn't feeling very special at all. In doing so, she taught me some lessons beyond reading and writing and arithmetic. They are lessons that are still with me today, lessons that I try to apply in my daily life.

Thank you, Mrs. Kaufman.

The little girl with the worn-out shoes and the low self-esteem has grown up to be a successful woman, with a good deal of education, a challenging and rewarding career, a wide array of interests. The attention a caring teacher showed that sad child, the light she shined into a pretty gloomy existence, helped immensely in that eventual transformation. There would be bumps along the way, low spots in the road from there to here, but through it all some of the things learned that first year in the Douglass School helped sustain me.

Thank you, Mrs. Kaufman.

Mine was a poor family, and there were a lot of us, which meant what little there was got spread around all the more thinly. Eventually there would be seven children in the family.

I was the fourth.

The first house I can remember was on McKinley Street, in the notorious "Black Bottoms" section of Gary. My hometown was then, and to some extent still is today, a highly segregated place. Although this was the mid-1950s and one of the major industrialized cities of the Midwest, in my mind's eye the Bottoms was like something out of the rural South around the turn of the century. The streets were unpaved and turned to mud during heavy rains. Some of the properties were small farms, with hogs and chickens and other animals.

Many of the people raised virtually all their food on the land around the homes.

The Black Bottoms acquired its name as a result of the color of the people who lived in that section of the city and its proximity to swamp land near the shores of Lake Michigan. I can remember my brothers, the oldest and most rambunctious of them in particular, going out into the swamps and catching snakes on purpose, coming back with leeches attached to their bodies by accident.

The first house in my memory had no indoor plumbing. A pump in the kitchen supplied running water. Our baths were taken in a big round tub filled with pump water my mother had heated on the stove.

Our bathroom was an outhouse.

My family moved to a house on Polk Street when I was six years old. It was from this house that I would attend the Douglass School and meet Mrs. Kaufman.

Some of the families in our new neighborhood were fairly well off, at least compared with the folks back in the Black Bottoms. Some may have even owned their own houses.

While the move represented a step up for my family, it was only a marginal one; we lived in the basement of someone else's home.

A girl close to my age, Janice, lived in the house across the street. She was one of five children, but her family was much better off than mine. The father worked in one of the steel mills or had some other factory job, and he provided well for his family.

One of my good friends in the neighborhood, Davida, was the daughter of a single parent. Her mother had moved in with a sister and brother-in-law, who had a girl of their own, Gail. It seemed to me like these two girls got everything they ever wanted: new clothes, new toys, new skates. These were things of which I could only dream. They seemed spoiled, at least in comparison with us.

Mine was not a very happy family, nor a very cohesive one. To put it plainly, my father was abusive toward my mother. This was not a secret kept within the confines of the basement in which we lived. People in the neighborhood were aware of this. Relatives of ours who lived far away from Gary were aware of this.

It seemed as though the whole world knew.

I always felt as if people were looking down on us. Kids can be so very cruel. They poke fun at the children whose parents fight, and this only adds to the misery.

My dad was hardly ever home, but when he was, there was trouble. He worked at an auto parts factory. He also spent a lot of time on the streets.

I think my father was a sort of wild child who just never really grew up.

Mrs. Kaufman brought some joy into my unhappy, poverty-stricken existence.

Thank you, Mrs. Kaufman.

I remember her as being very pretty. She was a young teacher, or seemed that way to me. She was, perhaps, in her middle twenties. I thought of her as being so very smart. She seemed to like me, and I was greatly encouraged by this. I always liked reading and writing, any kind of learning.

Mrs. Kaufman allowed me to stay after school, and even invited me to help her grade papers. This made me feel so very special. I thought, "I must be pretty smart, that she would pick me to grade papers."

I didn't mind staying after class. I didn't mind it at all.

It was nicer than going home. Honestly it was.

My mother didn't seem to miss me when I stayed late. There were so many of us, and she was so very busy preparing meals and doing other things around the house. Going home meant sometimes arriving in the middle of an argument between my parents, or listening to my father complain. He complained about the things the children did and the things we didn't do.

It was always something.

If I went home when he wasn't there, it would only be to find chores waiting, nothing that was very exciting, nothing that was very interesting.

Nothing that would earn me a shiny dime.

That's what Mrs. Kaufman paid me to help her grade papers. Shiny dimes. My first wages.

Those dimes meant a great deal to me. They represented independence. I can remember asking my parents for a nickel or a dime, and more often than not they didn't have one to give me.

In the neighborhood around Polk Street, several people had candy stores set up in their houses. I could buy a lot of penny candy with those shiny dimes Mrs. Kaufman paid me for my assistance.

When I started attending the first grade at Douglass School, Mrs. Kaufman could probably tell that I was unhappy. She probably saw me as one of the poorer children in the neighborhood.

The homemade dresses, sewn by my older sister, would have been one hint.

But the real tip-off was the shoes.

Mine were not merely worn out, but actually ragged. I would always have to wear a pair until there were holes in the bottom, and then long after that. I can remember starting out many days by putting cardboard in the bottoms of my shoes to keep from ruining my socks. I can vividly recall coming home with my younger sister and our mother ordering us to take off our socks and wash them in the bathroom sink with a bar of Ivory soap so that we could wear them again the next day.

Mrs. Kaufman had to notice that my shoes were literally falling apart, but she never mentioned it.

She never even mentioned it when, one day, she brought a pair of shoes to school and gave them to me.

Mrs. Kaufman was careful to wait until classes were done and no other students were around to give me the shoes. She did this so I wouldn't be so embarrassed. She told me they had been purchased for her niece, but that they were now too small for her. She did this to spare me embarrassment as well. I could tell that the shoes were new; they had never been worn by her niece.

In spite of Mrs. Kaufman's efforts, I was still a little embarrassed, somewhat ashamed that she had noticed the condition of the shoes I had been wearing.

And yet, it was such a wonderful gesture. It has stuck with me all these years, and touches my heart still.

Thank you, Mrs. Kaufman.

It is my firm conviction that events from our past stick in our minds for a reason. I believe the many kindnesses shown by my first grade teacher remain with me today because of the things they taught me, the important lessons learned. I early-on gained a lasting work ethic as a result of earning money for helping to grade papers in that after-school classroom. I know, because I found out from Mrs. Kaufman, that all of us have the power to affect the lives of others. It is so very easy to ruin someone's day with a cruel word, a thoughtless act. It is equally easy to make someone's day with a kind word, a thoughtful gesture. Mrs. Kaufman's example forces me to concentrate on the ways in which I can make life better for other people.

Mrs. Kaufman gave me much more than a new pair of shoes, a safe and comfortable place to be after school, all those shiny dimes. She gave me love and understanding and a feeling of my own worth.

Thank you, Mrs. Kaufman.

The little girl with the holes in her shoes grew up to be president and chief executive officer of the first and, until January 2001, the only minority operated, fully certified community mental health center in Indiana.

She remembers you, Mrs. Kaufman, and she is grateful to this day.

Power Point 1:
■ ■ ■ ■ ■ ■ ■ ■ ■ ■ ■ ■ ■

Build supportive relationships. It is important for your personal success that you surround yourself with people who care about your well-being and who desire to help you move ahead. The relationship should be built on respect and trust. Supportive relationships are a great source of guidance and comfort. They teach, nurture, and provide a good foundation for you to build on. Supportive relationships require reciprocity to be most effective.

CHAPTER TWO

Hand-Me-Down World

✤

Eyesight is what you see in front of you. Vision is what you see down the road.

— Victor M. Woods

When you're the fourth of seven children in a poor family, "new" doesn't enter into the picture very often. Hardly at all, really.

For example, I was the only one in the family who never got a brand new bicycle.

In a curious way, it's made me a better person, but at the time it was hard to take, just another part of the overall emptiness felt by so many middle children of large families.

My older sister got a brand new bike, probably purchased with money provided by my grandfather. I remember my two brothers proudly showing off their new bicycles when they got them, and even my two younger sisters eventually received new two-wheelers, but when it came to me the money was never there at the right time.

One by one, all my friends in the neighborhood in Gary, Indiana, got new bicycles.

What eventually came my way was my older sister's bicycle, a hand-me-down. It was an older model Schwinn, a clunky thing that was so big and bulky I could barely ride it. This wasn't at all like the slick, sleek new bikes of my friends. It probably weighed more than I did. I was just so very embarrassed to be seen struggling along on that bicycle.

The same thing held true for the most part when it came to clothes. My older sister, ten years my senior, knew how to sew and we even had a sewing machine of our own. Just before the start of each school year, she would sew three or four dresses for me as well as for my other sister who was then in school. Other than socks and underwear, none of our clothes came from the store.

One cold morning when I was nine years old, my mother tried to send me to school wearing an old and ugly jacket that had belonged to one of my brothers. It didn't fit at all, and it was obviously a boy's garment. I was mortified.

It was the first time I ever skipped school. I loved learning and I loved being in class; it was a welcome respite from the turmoil I often found at home, so for me to play hooky was a sign of just how upset I was.

My mother was so very busy, coping with the abuse she received from my father and trying to see to the basic needs of all of us, that she had very little individual time for her children. About the only one at home who tried to make me feel at all special was my older sister, Pam. She was more of a mother figure, really, but she had her own life to live. In my earliest memories my sister was already a teenager, but she did take some time to pay attention to her younger brothers and sisters. When she finally decided to move out on her own in the mid-1960s, to take a job in Chicago and share an apartment with a girlfriend, I was devastated. It felt like being deserted. Other than my younger sister, Denise, Pam was the only one I could talk to in the family.

I was very hurt by this perceived abandonment.

We learn to walk by falling down and picking ourselves back up. Somehow, in the process of dealing with my grief over the departure of my older sister, I learned to pick myself up emotionally. I began to realize it was probably not wise to depend too much on others for happiness. It is in many ways a mistake to rely on others, particularly for the kinds of internal things over which we ultimately have the power.

Feeling sorry for myself wasn't accomplishing very much, and I began to understand it was up to me to make the changes in my life necessary to know some measure of pleasure.

If I didn't want my entire existence to be nothing but hand-me-downs, I had to prepare myself so that I could direct what happened in my life.

In order to do this, we must sometimes be willing to make sacrifices. That is so much easier to say than it is to do. These sacrifices can be in the form of not getting something we really want, but they can just as easily take the form of getting rid of something that is holding us back.

Like my sister finally separating from her family and moving in with that friend in Chicago.

Most people, and I am no exception, are attracted to the quick fix. We want instant gratification. But the things that are really worth having almost always take time to obtain. A good career, a proper education, a solid marriage. None of these things happen overnight.

They require work and they require effort and they require dedication.

For me, achieving the worthwhile things in life required visualizing a goal and then taking the steps to reach that goal. What kept me going was knowing that one day I would get there.

I remember as a young adult, in my early twenties, that so many of my friends had gotten out of high school and found jobs in mills or factories. Talk about instant gratification! These jobs paid top dollar at that time, what seemed like a fortune to many of us. Soon my friends had new cars, nice apartments, good clothes. Some even had homes of their own, which for many of the people from my neighborhood was a kind of ultimate dream.

It all looked so good from the outside, and I was surely on the outside.

By that time I was already divorced. I had my children to care for and at times this forced me to go on public assistance. There never seemed to be enough money for the things we needed, let alone the things we might want. On occasion we didn't even have enough to eat, and knowing your kids are hungry, and feeling hungry yourself, is one miserable experience.

Oh, I tried to get a job in a steel mill. I tried to find work in a can factory, in any of the industrial operations that were then going strong in Gary. I must have filled out a dozen job applications, easily.

But I never got hired.

After holding down a series of part-time jobs for brief periods, I finally found full-time employment as a psychiatric attendant at Beatty Memorial Hospital. My mother worked there and helped me get the job. This turned out not to be the sort of thing for which I was cut out. The "bedpan brigade" was not for me.

I knew that I could do better.

I had a very profound experience while working at Beatty Memorial. Probably because I so disliked the job, I was frequently late for work. My immediate supervisor counseled me regarding this on several occasions. During one such talk, I became very defensive and was less than kind with my remarks to the woman. Later that day, her superior took me aside and asked what had led me to use that tone with my supervisor. I shrugged and said I was angry.

The boss of my boss looked at me.

"You're always angry," she said.

Sometimes we need to hear it from the outside to know what's going on inside of us. I realized right away the woman's assessment was absolutely accurate. I thought all the rest of that day about what she had said, and I continued to think about it for several days. I came to the conclusion that "always angry" is no way to go through life, and resolved to change my attitude. I began working on doing just that.

I visualized it, and began working toward that goal.

I also decided, perhaps in some way as part of the entire internal changing process, that I wanted to go to college. This was based only in part on how much I hated my job. In fact, in a strange way my place of employment had a great influence on me in terms of wanting to continue my education. At Beatty Memorial Hospital I was exposed to any number of professional people, not only doctors and nurses but also teachers and social workers. You'd better believe that I took notice of the fact none of these people had to clean up bodily fluids or empty bedpans.

I began to aspire to be just like them. I wanted to be looked upon as an intelligent person, someone worthy of respect. Someone worthy of admiration.

I visualized it, and set out to achieve that goal.

I applied for financial aid and was accepted at Indiana University Northwest. I majored in public administration with a concentration in criminal justice. I was a very studious student and completed my bachelor's degree with a 3.5 grade point average in three and a half years.

Meanwhile, the mills began to close. The factories began laying people off. The kinds of jobs that had been the backbone of Gary's economy were blowing away like dust in the wind.

A lot of my friends had to sell their nice cars. Some had to give up their homes. More than a few had to move back to the sort of neighborhood and style of living they thought they had escaped for good.

I, on the other hand, had my college degree. With it, I had gotten a pretty good job with decent pay.

The tables had definitely turned.

My friends, who had gotten the things they wanted practically right away, were now having these things taken away from them. I, who hadn't gotten many material things, but who instead had gotten an education, wound up with something no one can ever take away from me.

Sometimes I try to imagine what would have happened if I had ever gotten one of those jobs I applied for at the mills and the factories. I ask myself: With all that physical labor, with working different shifts, with the children to care for, would I have still gone to college?

My answer is: Probably not.

It has occurred to me that a higher power was looking down and saying, "No, that's not the kind of job you should get. You were meant to do some other work."

By the way, I could buy myself any kind of bicycle imaginable.

I think I'll wait until I find just the right one.

Power Point 2:

■ ■ ■ ■ ■ ■ ■ ■ ■ ■ ■ ■

Develop a Plan for Your Life. Developing a plan allows you to take control of your life. It forces you to think beyond today and to visualize where you want your life to take you. It gives you the freedom to choose the road that will bring you the most happiness and contentment. Developing a plan and having the discipline to carry it out is your key to personal success.

CHAPTER THREE

The 'Enemies' List

❦

In times of difficulty, you may feel that your problems will go on and on, but they won't. Every mountain has a top. Every problem has a life span. The question is, who is going to give in first, the frustration or you?

— Dr. Robert H. Schuller

Consider:

- As a child, I had exceptionally low self esteem; I just didn't think much of me.

- I came from a turbulent and abusive family situation made all the worse by the fact that we lived for a time in abject poverty.

- An unwed mother as a teenager, I had to complete high school on my own; no cap and gown for me.

- I entered into a bad marriage as a result of the pregnancy. It didn't last long, and by the time I was twenty years old I was a divorced single mother of two.

- A series of dead-end part-time jobs led to a full-time job that I absolutely hated.

- I was chronically late for work, and I had a very bad attitude toward my job and my employers.

Those were the facts of my life.

These are also the facts:

- I am currently the president and chief executive officer of a community mental health center in my hometown of Gary, Indiana. As such, I am one of only three women and, until January 2001, the only African-American who can make that claim in the state.

- I am also president of my own professional speaking, consulting and training firm.

- With two master's degrees already earned, I am working toward my doctorate.

- As an inspirational and motivational speaker, I have made appearances around the country and internationally.

A lot of people faced with the same or similar circumstances of my background and upbringing might see themselves as victims. I know I did. I viewed my family situation, my becoming pregnant, the bad marriages, the divorces, the detested jobs as a series of enemies arrayed against me.

In between that first set of facts and the second, something happened.

You see, I had met the enemy, and she was me.

Eventually, I was able to do something about this "enemy." Eventually, I was able to get her on my side, working for me.

But it certainly didn't seem that way when I was sixteen years old. This was a period in my life when I was very rebellious and also exceptionally unhappy. I was deeply dissatisfied with my home life and had an absolutely awful relationship with my father. My mother I viewed as being too weak-willed too dominated by my father, to be of any help. There was no other adult to whom I could turn with these feelings that raged within me.

I was looking for friendship, looking for love. I was looking for the things I was not getting at home, but in a misguided, immature way. I made a lot of mistakes in seeking these things.

One of those mistakes was becoming pregnant at sixteen.

My parents were, to say the least, not very happy about this development. They offered me little understanding. They made a painful situation even worse. My mother and father wanted me to get married right away, but this was opposed by the parents of the father of the child that was growing within me. Eventually, the boy and I took it upon ourselves to make the decision regarding marriage. I was in my sixth or seventh month when the ceremony was performed.

I gave birth to a beautiful baby girl.

The divorce, the seemingly inevitable divorce, did not become final until five years and another baby later, but the first of a series of breakdowns in the relationship occurred only six months after the wedding. We would get back together, only to break up again.

Eventually, I was almost completely on my own. The task of rearing the children fell almost entirely to me. My mother helped out some with occasional baby-sitting, but the father of my children offered practically no assistance at all.

This embittered me, but also toughened me in a way. I decided I didn't need him, that I was going to do this on my own.

On my own was a tough row to hoe. With the help of public assistance, I was able to rent relatively nice apartments, but these rarely contained very much furniture. I took what jobs I could find, but didn't like them very much. I quickly discovered I was not cut out to be a waitress, but still found myself doing just that on several occasions.

Conversations with my father were an endless series of, "I told you so." It was the last thing I needed to hear and seemingly the only thing he ever said. When even a modest amount of support from him would have made a major difference in how I felt about myself and my life, he would offer none, could offer none. He was always so very negative.

Once I left home to embark on the ill-fated marriage, I vowed that I was never going back. Keeping that vow was so very difficult with what felt like the entire weight of the world on my frail shoulders.

I suppose the worst time came for me when I was forced to stay with a girlfriend from high school, Toni. A single parent like me, she was living with her mother in an apartment in East Chicago. I had no other place to stay. There was barely enough money for formula and diapers for the baby. She had a bad rash as a result of wearing a wet diaper for longer than she should have.

One evening I decided to go home, but not to stay. I was going to leave the baby with my mother. I was going to admit I couldn't handle this and leave the problem in my mother's lap and go, I don't know where. I was simply going to drop off the baby.

At the last minute, I changed my mind. I couldn't do it. I never even told my mother what I had been planning to do.

It was awful.

In retrospect, I realize that there was a war going on inside of me, from my childhood through my adolescence and on into my early adult years. It was why I was so angry, why I was such a rebel. Even before I became pregnant, there were such low expectations of me, low expectations of where I would end up in life, that I was wracked with self-doubt. When the baby came along, that just added to the stereotypes I needed to fight against.

I fought against them.

I did so because a part of me wanted to excel. A voice inside my head demanded that I be successful. Part of me wanted a better life.

Part of me wanted to say to others, "You can't define me by your expectations. You can't define me through your limitations."

I guess that side of me won out.

I became the first member of my immediate family to enroll in college, although I don't recall receiving very much, if any, encouragement to do so.

Although my parents, both of them high-school dropouts, were set on each of their children completing high school, going beyond that was simply not in the cards. In fact, in my neighborhood, someone going to college was so out of the ordinary, I felt uncomfortable talking about it once I had started.

I just kept telling myself, that voice inside my head kept insisting, "This is what you want." I began to feel more and more that in order to be happy in my life I had to determine what it was I wanted and then move toward that goal.

I had to be the one setting the agenda for myself.

It really wasn't that difficult, not once I had made up my mind that I wanted to go to college. I simply focused everything on making certain I got it done.

That might sound easy to say and difficult to do, but it wasn't, not really, not when I harvested all my energy and channeled it into this specific direction.

I applied for and received financial aid and went through an orientation program at the local campus of Indiana University.

I asked a lot of questions of practically everyone I thought might be of help as I set about becoming a college student. There was a man with whom my mother worked at a psychiatric hospital who was also a college student, and I had mom ask him about getting money to pay for an education. He recommended a place right in my hometown of Gary that provided assistance to people in filling out financial aid applications.

Finding out that my application had been successful was an absolutely wonderful feeling, tinged with a little bit of disbelief and no small amount of fear. Orientation was only a month away.

I began to question myself.

Did I belong among college students? After all, I only had a GED. I hadn't gotten to march up and receive my diploma like the rest of my high school classmates. There had been no cap and gown, no procession.

I knew I was ready, but wondered if I was truly ready. I knew I could do this, but wondered if I could really do this.

Even though I was barely twenty-one years old, one of my major fears was that I would show up for classes and be so much older than all the other students. After all, people went to college right out of high school, didn't they?

It turned out that at Indiana University Northwest when I started in 1974, people started their higher education at a variety of ages. Some of the students were easily twice my age, and I soon became comfortable among my new classmates.

My initial plan only included attending college long enough to get an associate's degree. However, the course work and the classes went so much better and time went by so much faster than I had anticipated that, by the time I had enough credits for an associate of arts, I thought, "Why stop now?"

While a lot of major decisions were behind me at the point when I first enrolled in college, many still loomed, and I was completely unprepared for some of them.

Selecting a major was one of them.

You see, my entire goal had been to get a college degree. In what area of study, I had no idea.

I had not, to that point in my life, been exposed to a lot of different careers, and had not been through anything like actual career counseling. My background led me to believe that there were really only two professions to which women could aspire: teaching and nursing. Some distant relatives on my father's side were in the teaching profession and, it seemed to me, that field was more open than many to African Americans.

That might be something to shoot for, I thought.

However, in speaking with a cousin of my father's who was a teacher, Ulysses, I learned that it was not a good career to choose at that particular time. The cousin did impress upon me that I should go ahead and get my college degree. He told me, and it is so very true, that once I got that degree it was something no one could ever take away from me. It was something I would have with me for the rest of my life.

Nursing, then, seemed the clear choice, but then I recalled how unpleasant my experiences had been working in the same psychiatric hospital as my mother, and that seemed like no choice at all.

In fact, I was undecided about a major until I was almost entering my junior year. Then I chanced to come into contact with the dean of Public and Environmental Affairs at Indiana University Northwest, and it sounded like an interesting area of study. He explained that although Public and Environmental Affairs was its own major, there were many different disciplines within it. I eventually majored in public administration with a concentration in criminal justice, the latter as a result of knowing some people who had worked in the local juvenile justice system.

My father used to call me "stubborn." I prefer to think of myself as directed. I was certainly that when it came to applying myself to my studies. I did almost nothing else. My life was work, classes and then home to study and care for the children. I almost never went out with my friends. I knew that I could not have an active social life and see to the needs of my babies while completing college.

Work and school. That was my life.

I knew that there were better things coming, rewards awaiting me down the road for this dedication and determination. But at the same time I sort of enjoyed this studious existence. There was sanctuary for me in going home and reading my textbooks, writing my papers. I was beginning to think in different ways and starting to expand my horizons. Just as at one point I had been a young woman whose only goal had been a college degree, now I was someone with a definite major and a specific area of concentration within that major.

By going to summer school every year, I received my bachelor's degree in three and a half years while maintaining a 3.5 grade point average.

I was absolutely elated. Goal achieved. Mission accomplished.

So many people in my life had told me, directly or indirectly, that I could not do this or that or the other thing. So many people had tried, directly or indirectly, to get me to lower my expectations, that it made this achievement all the more special.

The entire time I was in college, my father kept saying that I would never graduate. As I continued earning credits toward my degree, he then complained that I was not spending enough time with my children. With him it was always something negative.

But I was determined. I saw I was going to do this. I said no one was going to stop me.

Not even myself.

Earning that degree opened a lot of doors for me, and it also did a world of good for my ego.

Power Point 3:

■ ■ ■ ■ ■ ■ ■ ■ ■ ■ ■ ■

Embrace Obstacles. The obstacles you face, the challenges you are confronted with, can be some of your best teachers. Each time you are confronted with a difficult—seemingly impossible—situation, consider it a lesson in disguise. Use these times to your advantage. From them you can learn patience, tolerance, perseverance, and even creativity.

CHAPTER FOUR

Grandma's Hands

Love alone is capable of uniting living beings in such a way as to complete them, for it alone takes them and joins them by what is deepest in themselves.

— Unknown

As of this writing, my 95-year-old grandmother still walks everywhere she goes. She never learned to drive a car, and routinely refuses to accept rides from friends and family members.

"I've come this far by myself," she will say, "I may as well go the rest of the way."

Some of my grandmother's strength has helped me to come this far. I will be keeping her in mind as I go the rest of the way.

She is my paternal grandmother, but isn't like my father very much at all. In fact, she does not have a very good relationship with either of her two children, both sons, although I know she loves them very much.

"Grandma," as we called her, is not and was not very demonstrative when it comes to showing affection. She's not big into hugging and kissing. She has a very matter-of-fact approach to life and is something of a disciplinarian.

It seems a harsh word picture, and hardly does the woman justice. For in her quiet, steadfast way she always made us know how much she cared for us, how much she loved us. I, who needed that kind of care and was seeking that sort of love, basked in this warmth.

Not only did my grandmother not get along that well with my father, but also she tended to side with me when he was saying negative things about me, accusing me of being stupid or saying I had done something wrong.

"You leave that child alone!" my grandmother would say. "She's just fine. She's OK."

It was music to my ears. It was something I needed to hear.

At times, grandma would take me aside and say, "There's nothing wrong with you."

Oh, did I need to hear those words!

Her husband, my grandfather, died when I was about nine years old. I loved him very much and remember him with great fondness. He used to come over and do things with and for his grandchildren. He would bring us a watermelon or take us to the store to buy candy. We got some of the attention from him that we lacked from his son, our father.

In going to visit our grandparents, I seem to recall grandma all the time fussing at "grand daddy." She would chastise him about coming home late the previous evening, or not being on time for dinner. In some ways I felt sad for my grandfather, that he was the subject of so much complaining from his wife.

But that was just our grandmother. She didn't, and doesn't, bite her tongue. When she has something to say, and she often does, grandma doesn't hesitate to say it. You always know where she stands now, and I always knew where she stood when I was just a child. That was part of what made her so special to me; grandma bothered to tell me her views on things, she felt I was worthy of being aware of her opinions.

Grandma had this message to tell me, and she did so in word and deed: You need not seek the approval of others, not as long you have confidence in yourself.

My grandmother would have been in her early fifties when grand daddy passed, and although she was a very attractive woman, tall and slender with long, lovely hair, she never remarried. In her words, she "didn't want to be bothered with men anymore."

That was grandma.

She was in many ways a woman ahead of her time: fiercely independent when that was definitely the exception, not the rule.

I always viewed my mother as being very weak, and I know how unkind that sounds. Perhaps this was to some extent solely in comparison with grandma. My mother never stood up to my father, even when she had to know his harshness toward the children was wrong. As a result I was not very close to my mother, not very forgiving of her weaknesses. Even though today I can better understand why she was the way she was, given her circumstances and the society of which she was a product; it's difficult to look back and not think about how much better our lives might have been if just on occasion my mother stood up to my father.

Grandma stood up to him all the time. And by not re-marrying after the death of my grandfather, she showed that she did not have to have someone to take care of her, as my mother seemed to do.

My grandmother didn't have a lot of money, but she fended for herself rather than relying on others. She would baby-sit for people in the community, local lawyers and other professionals.

As I mentioned, grandma never learned to drive and walks everywhere she goes or takes a public bus when she has to travel longer distances.

Although she was no doubt somewhat disappointed in me when I became pregnant while still in high school, my grandmother never said one negative word about the situation to me.

She was probably very unhappy, but was careful not to add to my already considerable misery.

When I decided to enroll in college to better myself and make a brighter future for my children, grandma was about the only member of the family, along with my mother, to offer real encouragement.

She was pleased that one of her grandchildren had that kind of ambition, and when I graduated she was so very, very proud of me.

To this day my grandmother doesn't hesitate to tell her friends and acquaintances about all the degrees I have earned and my professional accomplishments.

She takes pride in me and that makes me feel good about myself and some of the decisions I made.

She was and is so very strong-willed.

I think I have a lot of my grandmother in me, and that makes me proud.

Power Point 4:

■ ■ ■ ■ ■ ■ ■ ■ ■ ■ ■ ■ ■

Fill Your Life with Love. Love heals, it inspires, it comforts. You must truly learn to love yourself. Self-hatred is spawned from self-doubt, self-denial, and self-despair.

When you begin to love *you* unconditionally, you can then begin to share the gift of love with others.

CHAPTER FIVE

Degrees of Difference

❧

Everyone has inside him a piece of good news. The good news is that you don't yet realize how great you can be! How much you can love! How much you can accomplish! And what your potential is!

— Anne Frank

Flipping burgers.

"You want fries with that?"

As a young woman struggling to make ends meet and raise my children with the kind of jobs I could get with my GED, I ended up flipping my share of burgers and asking that famous question over and over. These were often the only jobs I could find, the only work for which I appeared to be qualified. I loathed that kind of work.

As a young woman about to receive a bachelor of arts degree in Public Administration from Indiana University Northwest, I was offered not one but two full-time positions.

Neither of them involved flipping or fries.

One of these was in the juvenile probation system in my native Lake County, Indiana. It held out the possibility of long-term employment and fit in nicely with my area of concentration in college, which was Criminal Justice. I would have been a part of a major reform of the entire juvenile justice system in Lake County.

The other position was only a summer job, and it was in Crown Point, Indiana, about 20 miles from my home. The temporary opening was for a supervisor of the Comprehensive Employment and Training Act Summer Youth Employment Program. There were no assurances this would be a stepping stone to anything of a more permanent nature.

I took the job that offered the greater risks, and also the greater challenges, and that has made all the difference.

The job of probation officer had its attractions, over and above being a permanent position. A new juvenile court judge had taken over in Lake County, and she was determined to bring reform to a system mired in old ways. Most of the probation officers on the staff when she stepped in had been there for ages. The judge wanted to replace many of them, and she had two reasons. For one thing, she felt younger probation officers would be better able to understand the youthful offenders who would be their clients. For another, most of the existing probation officers had gotten their jobs through political patronage, and few if any had college degrees. The new judge wanted to instill greater professionalism in the system, and one of the ways in which she wanted to do this was by hiring people who had a higher level of education than the current staff members.

Three things held me back from leaping at this opportunity to take what I had learned in class and apply it in the field.

One involved a tragedy: Earlier in 1977, the year I graduated, a young female probation officer in Lake County had been murdered. She was abducted outside a neighborhood grocery store by two young men. While driving around with her in her car, they found the officer's badge. Realizing they were in even greater trouble than if they had simply kidnapped a civilian, the two panicked. They shot and killed the young woman in an attempt to cover up their crime.

Secondly, serving as a juvenile probation officer would have required me to carry a gun. I was not at all comfortable with that aspect of the job.

Finally, though, I was drawn to the CETA position because of one word in the job description: "supervisor." I would be my own boss. It was a lot of responsibility, but after all, wasn't that why I had gone to college?

There was a definite appeal in the idea of helping young people get started in the world of work through the federal program, and I was taken by the personnel aspects of the position. While at Indiana University Northwest, I had served an internship through the School of Public and Environmental Affairs. This involved work with the job classification system in Lake County government, including writing job descriptions and assigning pay grades.

The CETA Summer Youth Employment Program in Crown Point involved working with employers to develop summer jobs for young people, placing youth in these jobs and then monitoring their progress following placement. I was in charge of the job development counselors, who went out to the work sites and met with the potential employers. In addition to keeping tabs on these people, I also worked with the employers to make certain the jobs that were developed under the program met the criteria established by the federal act and that they were properly listed with the state Division of Employment.

I learned a lot, and quickly, about supervising people, relating to them and seeing to it that they got their jobs done. I learned some hard lessons about not becoming too close to the people under my supervision, because of the ways in which others might perceive this.

I somewhat surprised myself by absolutely thriving in this job. The work really bolstered my self esteem. I finally felt like I was measuring up, finally had something to offer.

Of course, being offered two good jobs, when there had been a time not so long ago when I could find none, had done a lot for my ego. It made me feel good. I remember saying to myself, "Maybe things are finally looking up for you."

I gained extra confidence in myself not only because I had a choice of jobs, but also by succeeding in the one I decided upon.

I didn't let myself dwell upon the fact that the CETA job was going to end once summer was over. For one thing, the work kept me quite busy. More importantly, my newfound confidence had me convinced that something would come along. I had my degree and would eventually find work that was part of a career path.

Besides, I could always flip burgers. You see, I would have known that was only temporary, until something better came along, as opposed to being the best I could expect.

I was also able to experience, in that first assignment out in the real world, the ways in which my college education applied. For example, the language, or perhaps a better term is the jargon, spoken by those in the field of employment was familiar to me and really helped in that first job. I know that sounds like a minor thing, but being knowledgeable about the terms used helped make me more confident and increased the confidence others had in me.

Also, some of the classes in management and supervision I had taken had provided me with a good theoretical framework. I was able to go over these theories in my mind as I dealt with the people I supervised and find ways in which, on an individual basis, they could be put into practice.

I am the kind of person who asks a lot of questions, particularly when I feel uncertain or need some direction. I have been fortunate enough throughout my life to latch on to certain people willing to act as mentors, to provide advice and guidance on how to handle certain situations. I don't know everything. I don't pretend to know everything. Being aware of this, I am able to seek out those who have worthwhile advice, and to listen to them.

As my time with CETA was drawing to a close, I spotted an ad in the local paper for an assistant personnel and payroll manager at the Hammond, Indiana, campus of Purdue University. I applied and was lucky enough to get an interview. I did well in the initial interview with the department manager, and subsequently with his boss. In those interviews I stressed my educational background, the fact that I had already begun studying for my masters, taking classes while working in the Summer Youth Employment Program. I pointed out that I had some personnel and labor relations classes under my belt from my undergraduate days, and I emphasized the ways in which my most recent experiences would help in this new position.

The job of assistant personnel and payroll manager involved recruiting potential employees for all but the management and faculty positions on the Calumet campus, which employed between 600 and 700 people. The assistant manager conducted initial screening interviews and then made referrals of qualified candidates to various department heads. Once these people held their own interviews and made the selection of applicants, the assistant manager then handled the paperwork involved in processing new employees.

The university officials were impressed with me, with what I had learned in college and what I had done upon graduating. I got the job.

In interviewing prospective candidates, I followed a system already in place for rating people on their presentation, their academic background and their job experiences. Using my own perceptions, I would rate them in comparison with one another. It was challenging initially, because this was all so new to me and I wanted to do a good job. I was very conscious of how much my referrals of potential employees reflected upon me, how good my judgment was, the quality of my decision making. Always in the back of my mind I was aware of the need to refer absolutely the best candidates because it was on this basis that my own job performance would be evaluated.

I did fairly well in this assignment, with one memorable exception. There was one gentleman who kept coming in and coming in to apply for jobs in the maintenance department. He had a very spotty employment record, frequently leaving previous positions after only a month or two. Often these were under less than favorable circumstances, nothing outrageous but nothing that reflected too well on him as a worker, either. Nonetheless, he kept coming in and coming in. I was impressed with his persistence, and finally passed his name along to one of the department heads. That manager complained to my boss who came to me and asked why I had done what I had done. I explained that the man seemed to sincerely want to work for us, and that he had been so persistent.

I came to realize it had been a bad decision on my part, that persistence is only part of the equation and that other factors must be weighed. I learned from that experience.

I remained in that position for about two years, during which I completed my first master's degree at Indiana University Northwest. By the time the two years were nearly up, I began to get a little bored with the job. The tasks that had been so challenging at first had become routine. I felt a need for new challenges and began looking for another job.

I saw an ad in the paper for an opening at the Tri-City Community Mental Health Center in East Chicago. It was for a personnel director. I decided to take a chance and applied for the position. I didn't hear anything for a while, but I kept calling to follow up on my application. The secretary to the director came to recognize my voice. She assured me my application had been received. These things take time, she said.

Time passed and I did indeed get called for an interview with the director. We connected right away. I was only twenty five at the time, and he was no more than five or six years older, so we were close in age. We talked about my experiences, what I wanted to do with my life, the kind of background from which I had come. Although I did not meet each and every qualification listed for the opening, he decided to take a chance on hiring me. Also, he was able to pay me less than someone with more experience, something I found out later on.

Tri-City Community Mental Health Center had not previously had a personnel director. In my new position, I had to put the entire system together from the ground up.

I was more than a little frightened as the enormity of my new assignment became apparent. All the newfound confidence deserted me in the face of such a daunting task. Was I really up to this?

In fact, I was so uncertain of myself that I started working at the Tri-City Community Mental Health Center while on temporary leave from Purdue to recover from minor surgery. It was something I probably should not have done, but I desperately felt the need for that crutch, to be able to fall back on something I did know in the event I fell flat on my face in the new job. There was no one to tell me how to do things. I had to learn entirely on my own.

My new boss was very supportive of me, and I needed every bit of that support. It was an awesome responsibility. The other department heads viewed me as a resource and would bring their personnel concerns to me. I had to provide consultations with them while at the same time trying to set up my own department.

A difficult situation was made all the worse because some of the duties I was taking over had been handled by a woman on the clerical staff. The director felt that all the existing and coming regulations regarding personnel required a greater degree of professionalism, but many on the staff at the center had a rapport with the woman. They were friends with her and resented me at first. I was someone who was going to come in and disrupt a comfortable situation. Some of my coworkers were not very cooperative at the outset.

After a time I began to ease into the routine of my new job and to become more familiar with what was required of me. It helped that I had been given an assistant who had been at the center for quite a while.

My personality also helped. I am not, to put it bluntly, someone willing to take a lot of crap from people. I stood up to some of those who made my tasks even more difficult, in particular an assistant director who didn't much care for me. We butted heads frequently. She often complained to our boss that I was not doing my job correctly, but I stood up for myself. My habit of asking a lot of questions helped. Whenever I lacked clear direction, I wasn't shy about asking for it.

At one point, as a result of this assistant director refusing to be pleased with a report I had done, my boss came into my office and we got into a shouting match. He began yelling at me in front of my assistant and with the door to the office open, too.

I yelled right back, because the complaints about my report were unreasonable ones.

After he had stormed out, I told my assistant, "Well, I guess I'll be looking for another job." But the next day, the director acted as if nothing had occurred between us. Our relationship was unchanged as a result of the argument. It turned out that our relationship was such that we could truly tell one another how we felt, even when this might involve a little shouting.

After I had been at Tri-City Community Mental Health Center for about four and a half years, the center acquired a nursing home. At about the same time, I learned of a job opening at the Gary Community Mental Health Center in my hometown. It involved the exact same duties and same pay as I was receiving at Tri-City. I applied for the position and was accepted.

When I told my boss this, he was very upset and tried to talk me out of it, but he knew that I was getting antsy in my current job, that I wanted to stretch, to do something different. A big going-away party was thrown for me at a nearby restaurant on a Friday. At the party, my boss came up to me and suggested strongly that I didn't really want to take the new job. What would I think, he asked, about going to work at the nursing home Tri-City had acquired? I would learn new things, he pointed out. I would be involved in hiring or rehiring the entire staff. It would be an entirely different business and a different environment. There were intriguing aspects to the proposal, but I was due to start my job at Gary Community Mental Health on Monday. Let me think about it, I told him.

My boss called me over the weekend and asked if I had thought about it. He then asked me to think about a raise of $10,000 a year if I took the nursing home assignment.

I had one of the worst weekends of my entire life. I couldn't sleep. Part of it was anger at my boss. It was so unfair of him to wait until the eve of my departure to make this offer. I mean, at my going-away party?

On Monday I started at my new job in Gary, but sat down with the director almost immediately and told her of the opportunity to remain with Tri-City. I told her I wanted to be honest with her and that I was seriously considering the offer.

"We really need you here," she said. "We really need you to straighten out our personnel department."

Here was another guilt trip.

I decided to stay at least a week, take that amount of time to figure out what was best for me. In that period, I began to see that I had stepped into a very troubled situation. Gary Community Mental Health was badly disorganized, in part due to interference and "micro-managing" by members of the board of directors. I told my new boss at the end of that first week that things were not working out. I called my old boss and said I wanted to come back. I also told him that while I would be returning all the presents from my going-away party, there were still bound to be some bad feelings about this. Let me worry about that, he said.

I became the assistant administrator of the nursing home, with far more responsibility than personnel. In fact, much of the day-to-day operation of the facility soon fell to me.

Since that was the case, I decided to get my license as a nursing home administrator. The process required six months, during which time I began to get a dimmer and dimmer view of what running nursing homes entailed. At about the time this disillusionment began to set in, my position at the nursing home was going to be eliminated.

I needed a job, even if it was flipping burgers.

I updated my resume, and one of the places to which I sent it was Gary Community Mental Health Center. To my astonishment, I was offered the job of quality assurance coordinator. Once again I was faced with doing something I had never done before in my life, but officials at the center must have felt I was qualified for the position. I took the job and then began to figure out what it required, what the director of the center wanted from the quality assurance coordinator. I met with others in the same or similar position at other facilities and viewed the systems they had in place.

Naturally, I asked a lot of questions.

After a time, the executive director of the center instituted a complete restructuring of the organization. As a result, I became director of administration, a position I would hold for the next five years.

I didn't always see eye-to-eye with my direct supervisor. He was, in addition to being my boss, also a state representative, and spent months at a time in the state capital. He seemed to pay more attention to his General Assembly duties but at the same time was unwilling to give up some of his decision-making authority. I began to realize he was a rather insecure individual. This was my first experience in which I learned nothing positive from my boss. At board meetings, he frequently deferred to me in responding to questions. I was doing an awful lot of work for which I was getting neither credit nor recognition.

I resolved to leave.

One of the board members, Sheridan Powell, with whom I had developed a good working relationship, was also on the board of directors of a nursing home. I had vowed not to return to that field, because it can be so thankless and difficult and is so heavily regulated. Nevertheless I listened when he told me how greatly troubled this nursing home was. He pointed out that I could hardly make the organization any worse, that practically anything I did would be an improvement.

Also, and this probably tipped me in favor of listening to him, the board member told me it was finally time I assumed the top position of an organization. It might help me in the long run, he said, and would certainly look good on my resume. Who knows, the man said, I might one day return to Gary Community Mental Health Center as the overall administrator.

With some reluctance, I accepted the nursing home position, but only on a one-year contract. Although great strides were made in improving the operation of the facility, a politically motivated decision eventually led to the closing of the home. I was invited to stay on during the closing but, as luck would have it, I didn't need to do so. Shortly before my one-year contract was up, I had hired a young man as marketing director for the nursing home. He came to us with a nursing home background in the for-profit sector. When the handwriting was on the wall in terms of our facility going out of operation, he turned to his previous employer for a job. In the course of his being hired back, I was introduced to some executives with the national firm. They were impressed with the way the nursing home was being run. How about, they asked, coming to work for them?

It seemed like a blessing out of the blue, but the job they had in mind was in Terre Haute, Indiana. I had never really left Gary for any extended period of time, and found myself filled with uncertainty at the prospect.

I had been dating my current husband, Chuck, for nearly five years. Although it was a good relationship, we had no plans to become engaged. In talking with him about what I should do, he commented that for someone facing the prospect of being unemployed I seemed remarkably unconcerned.

And I was. I knew I could find another job.

I could at least flip burgers.

The time came when I had to make a decision. My facility was being closed. I could not afford to sit around and wallow in self pity. I decided to see this as an opportunity.

I met my future husband for lunch to inform him of my decision. I had found a new job, I said.

"Where?" he asked. "In Atlanta?"

No, I told him. It was in Terre Haute, only two and a half hours away. We could continue to see one another on weekends. This was not an opportunity which I could afford to pass up. The salary was good. My moving expenses would be paid. The for-profit corporation was a leader in the field.

He accepted my decision, but I could tell he was less than thrilled.

The next day he came by to take me to a movie. On the way, he said he wanted to stop at a jewelry store where my sister worked to drop off some watches to be repaired. My sister waited on us. She asked what brought us to the store.

"Actually," Chuck said, "we're here to get an engagement ring."

He had been married before, back when he was in college. He appeared to be one of those men who truly enjoyed the single life. I think he was reluctant to get married again. But the prospect of my moving away made a big difference to him. I accepted his proposal on the condition that we set a date for the wedding, and soon. This was not going to be one of those permanent engagements.

On New Year's Eve 1994, we were married in Lake Tahoe.

I worked at the nursing facility in Terre Haute for two years. During my time there, the home received one of the company's most prestigious awards, the "E Award," for our outstanding performance in meeting licensing requirements. The award brought bonuses and incentives for both myself and my employees.

I returned to Gary on the weekends, and spent long hours on the road every Tuesday afternoon and evening making the 200-mile round trip to take classes for another master's degree, this one from the University of Chicago's School of Social Services Administration. I had decided it was high time to explore the clinical side of the human services field, in particular the area of mental health.

After two years, I grew exceedingly weary of my commute on weekends. I looked for and found a job closer to home, as administrator for a nursing home in Valparaiso.

I was only there six months, before I made another career move.

It wasn't flipping burgers.

Power Point 5:

■ ■ ■ ■ ■ ■ ■ ■ ■ ■ ■ ■ ■

Don't sell yourself short. Believe in yourself and your ability to achieve success in life. You are capable of accomplishing much more than you can ever imagine. When you underestimate your potential, you confine yourself to a life of mediocrity. Prepare yourself emotionally and intellectually to take on new challenges. The rewards can be staggering.

CHAPTER SIX

Career Crossroads

❧

*The reason most people never reach their goals is that they
don't seriously consider them as believable or achievable.*

– Denis Waitley

Who knows?

When Sheridan Powell, a member of the board of directors at the Gary Community Mental Health Center, approached me about taking over as administrator of a nursing home where he was also on the board, he employed a number of different arguments to sway me. He had a lot of convincing to do, too. I was very reluctant to return to the nursing home field.

Although nursing homes provide a valuable service in our society, they tend not to be much fun to run. Even the best of nursing homes, those with proper funding and highly dedicated employees, present any number of headaches and heartaches to the overall head of the organization. And it should be pointed out that few nursing homes enjoy these favorable factors.

So Sheridan Powell had an uphill climb when he sought to change my mind.

At the time, I was on my second go-round at Gary Community Mental Health. My previous experience there had been as personnel director. It was but a one-week stint, during which I realized the center was simply too troubled an organization for me to tackle at that time. Several years later, with more administrative experience under my belt, I had come back to GCMHC as quality assurance coordinator.

Now, one of the center's board members was trying to persuade me to become administrator of a county nursing home. I listened; keeping an ear open to opportunity is always wise. But I was initially very uncertain about the wisdom of taking this position.

Mr. Powell pointed out that I would be escaping a situation in which I was frequently at odds with my direct supervisor, a situation in which I was often doing his work for him but not receiving the credit and where he was too insecure to listen to anyone's suggestions on how he could make the organization successful.

The board member also employed the argument that it was high time I assumed the top administrative position of an organization. My career had been heading in this direction, he suggested. I was ready to make the move and here was an opportunity to do so.

It would certainly look good on my resume, Sheridan Powell said.

"Who knows?" he added. "Maybe one day you'll come

back to Gary Community Mental Health as the overall administrator."

I chuckled at that. It seemed like the least likely of possibilities for my future.

Nonetheless, I let his arguments sway me and became administrator of the county nursing home. I did my level best to bring improvements to the operation of the home, and did so in many instances, until a political decision was made to shut down the operation.

I found a job with a private sector operator of nursing homes, working in Terre Haute, Indiana, while commuting to my home in Gary on weekends and to Chicago one night a week to continue my studies for an additional master's degree. Eventually tiring of all this driving, I looked for and found a job as administrator of yet another nursing home in the Gary area.

I was in that position for six months when I received a call one day from none other than Sheridan Powell. He was still on the board of directors of Gary Community Mental Health.

He asked me how I would like to come back to work there, this time as chief executive officer.

I didn't think I would like that at all. I knew, as only a former insider could, of the ongoing history of organizational problems at GCMHC. I was aware of its frequent financial difficulties, of the conflicts between board members and the staff, of its bad reputation in the community and its poor image within the field of community mental health. The more I thought about it, the more positive I became that this was not the move for me.

"Absolutely not," I told Mr. Powell.

"What would it take to change your mind?" he asked right back.

First and foremost, I replied, there would have to be changes made in the makeup of the board. Some of the existing members would have to go and new people brought on board who understood the role of a board of directors and their proper relationship with those on the center's staff. There would be no more of the micro managing of the operation for which some of the board members were famous.

I would accept the position only with the assurances that I would have the authority to run the organization as it needed to be run.

"I think we can do that," Sheridan Powell assured me.

It had been the furthest thing from my mind that I would ever return to Gary Community Mental Health Center in the top spot. I did know that I wanted to be CEO of some large organization, preferably a community mental health center.

As far back as 1981, when I took my first job in the field as personnel director at Tri-City Community Mental Health Center in East Chicago, I had been interested in not only the administrative side of such operations but also the clinical side. Lots of clinicians worked at Tri-City, several of them in management positions that brought me in contact with them. I always felt that these social workers, psychologists, psychiatrists and others had a special professional bond with one another because they shared this in-depth knowledge of a specific subject. It seemed to me they believed that only a clinician could truly understand clinical issues, and it also seemed to me that perhaps they were right.

I am the sort of person who does not like to feel inadequate in any situation, so this rankled. From that early experience in community mental health on, it was always in the back of my mind that I might like to explore the clinical side of the equation.

When I took the quality assurance coordinator job at Gary Community Mental Health, it seemed like a good time to do just that. Students from various programs in the many disciplines employed at a mental health center often worked at GCMHC. When one of the instructors from the University of Chicago paid a visit to the center to check on her students, I made it a point to seek the woman out. I asked her about the program at the U. of C. She said the program was badly in need of both women and minorities, that more females and people of color needed to be in the field.

I fit the bill on both counts.

I applied to the School of Social Service Administration and later to the graduate program in Health Administration and Policy at the University of Chicago, and was accepted. I began my studies in 1992 and received both my graduate certificate and my master's degree two years later.

I really felt like I needed to know the clinical side of things in order to have a complete understanding of the business. I had even thought I might perhaps do some therapy work on the side, but eventually decided that was not for me. I felt it was important to find this out, and even if I didn't become a therapist I would have a greater understanding of what they do by receiving some of the training to become one.

It's not rocket science. Some who have made counseling the focus of their entire professional careers might object to that statement, but there is a simple goal for therapy. It is really about helping people to make changes in their lives for the better. It is about getting them to make the best of the situations in which they find themselves, or discovering ways to alter those situations. It's about putting people in a position to become successful and be happy with their existence. Therapists must ask themselves, "How can I facilitate that process?" and move on from there.

There is really a lot of common sense involved.

I am not, of course, referring to those who require intensive therapy and medication in order to deal with severe mental illness. I am fully aware how devastating this can be.

But as is often the case with many things, those facing less serious mental health problems can, if assisted in analyzing their situation, come to see the obstacles they face. These can be psychological or emotional, or both.

Once these issues are brought to the forefront, however, people can often see ways in which to move beyond them, ways in which they can get on with their lives in spite of problems and difficulties.

I know, because I have done so.

It was therefore a more thoroughly educated and motivated woman who came back to Gary Community Mental Health Center, this time around as CEO.

I'm a person who loves challenges. I had gone knowingly into troubled situations and organizations in the past. I had accepted the task of turning these around, and more often than not I had succeeded.

I like working with people, managing people. I have been in many places that suffered from exceptionally poor management, poor supervisory relationships. Using my experience in the field and what I had learned from hundreds of textbooks, I have often been able to apply better principals and practices of management to bring about improvements and make corrections. The theories of management outlined in the books and discussed in classrooms provided me with something to fall back on, different perspectives, other ways to view situations.

All of this was going to be called upon if I was to right the ship known as the Gary Community Mental Health Center.

When I took over as chief executive officer, the center's annual budget was around $8 million. We probably had 160 people on the staff. The services included an inpatient unit, outpatient care for children, adolescents and adults; and addiction counseling. There were some residential programs for youth and two group homes for adults with serious mental illness. It was a pretty good range of mental health services, but it was being poorly and inadequately delivered to a community badly in need of such services.

In what seems like a massive contradiction, the center was increasingly faced with two major problems. On the one hand, we had a very long waiting list of people in need of our services. On the other hand, many of the normal referral sources such as the courts and Lake County Office of Family and

Children were opting to make us the place of last resort. They did so not only because of the long wait for service, but also because the quality of that service, once delivered, enjoyed a very poor reputation.

In such situations, a cooperative, understanding and supportive board of directors is crucial for the chief executive officer. I enjoyed a good relationship with a few of the existing board members. These were people with whom I felt I could work, and who would help me to build an effective team to do the job the center was supposed to do.

With the aid of these supportive board members, some of those less willing to embrace change were induced to move on. New people joined with an understanding of their role and a willingness to provide the CEO with the authority to make needed improvements.

Eventually I gained this understanding with the majority of the GCMHC board members: "You hired me, so support me and trust me, and together we can turn this thing around."

I was fortunate to have some really good staff members at the center, some people who had been there for a long time and were dedicated to doing their jobs, but were just looking for a little leadership. With the economic woes that had ravaged much of the industrial Midwest having hit Gary harder than most, people in the area were in serious need of the services a well-run community mental health center can offer. We had a ready market of clients right outside our doors. The center was housed in a lovely facility, a beautiful and substantial structure built in the early 1980s. While it had not been properly kept up and much of the furniture was slightly shabby, old and not very clean, the physical plant provided a good foundation on which to build.

Now it was up to us, and to me, to make good on what we had going for us as a community mental health operation.

I didn't go into the situation blindly. I knew from the outset that some on the senior management team had formed a little clique among themselves. I knew, further, that they had felt strongly one of their own should have become the chief executive officer. From notes and telephone calls I had received from some of my former colleagues at the center, I received a lot of advance advice: "Get rid of this one." "Move that one out." "Keep this person." "Fire that person."

I made it a point, however, not to bring any negative attitudes in with me when I walked through that door that first day as CEO. My feeling was: we start from here and we start fresh. Everyone has a chance to shine. We are all here to make this operation as successful as it possibly can be, to make our range of programs into an invaluable resource for the community. Show me that's what you want to do, and we'll go on from there.

I know a lot of CEOs come into an operation and set about installing their own people as the management team right away. I had no desire to do so.

I did bring a consultant in the community mental health field in with me, because I felt the need of some assistance in outlining what would need to be done in my first few months on the job. There were some daunting tasks, not the least of which was getting proper certification from the state as well as accreditation from a designated national accrediting body.

We were one of the few community mental health centers in the state not properly accredited. This was not merely something we should do as a matter of course, it was mandated by law.

We had to get this accomplished, and there was only about a year in which to do it.

The first step for me, therefore, was to put in place policies and procedures designed to result in our accreditation. Incredibly, there were virtually no policies and procedures in existence for the operation of the center and its programs. It became my number one priority to establish some standards and to make certain people met them.

From the outset it became obvious there were some on the staff who could not meet these standards. Even some who were capable of rising to the challenge of better, more accountable job performances did not like what I was attempting to do. They preferred the "good old days." They liked the way things had been handled when the board of directors interfered so much with the operation of the center and undermined the authority of the CEO. Some of these disgruntled employees complained to board members. One or two of those on the board attempted to make an issue of these complaints at their meetings. They were not permitted to do so, mostly because they were by then in the minority on the board.

In addition, I didn't permit board members to be in a position to exercise any authority over the day-to-day operations of the center. When I presented them with a new table of organization, I did not couch it in terms of being something "for your approval." I presented it as something "for your information." This was in keeping with my desire to separate the roles of board members from administrators.

Although some of the holdover board members didn't like this approach, and made some noise about their unhappiness, by and large they didn't interfere with me. Attempts at putting their noses in where they did not belong were blocked by the other board members, who emphasized that their role was to establish policy and provide oversight.

I insisted that members of my staff not contact board members directly with complaints. Such things had to go through me. It was my job, not that of board members, to deal with discontent among the employees.

This was something of a political gamble for me, but it paid off.

Those who did not like or could not adjust to the changes I was instituting began to move on. One of those displeased with my management approach attempted to do an end-run on me. The woman, who was the former medical director at the center, actually wrote her own employment contract and sought to put it before the board of directors. As written, it would have permitted her to report directly to the board, completely undermining my authority over this aspect of the center's operation. It would have created significant and unnecessary conflicts within the organization.

I had the contract removed from the agenda. I told board members I was not ready to make recommendations on such matters as yet, and that the former medical director's tentative contract had to be evaluated.

In the end, I declined to recommend extending a contract to the woman at all.

The chief financial officer left, as well.

In the end, I did not have to fire any of these management people who sought to protect their own little fiefdom within the center. They left of their own volition because I had set standards for behavior and performance that they simply could not or would not meet.

These departures, as welcome as they were in one way, posed major problems for me in another way. Because of the Gary Community Mental Health Center's generally poor reputation within the field, it was really difficult to find quality replacements. However, as I began to enjoy more and more success in getting supportive people appointed to the board of directors, I was able to reach out to former colleagues and offer them jobs with the assurance that things were being turned around at GCMHC. It was a hard sell in many instances, especially with anyone who had once been on the staff at the center. Things have changed, I had to assure them repeatedly. It's not the way it used to be.

Trust me, I said. I put my reputation on the line with these people.

Little by little, I began to build my own team of loyal employees who shared the goal of making the center fulfill its promise. I also began to promote from within those who were good team players and who wanted, had always wanted, to make the organization successful.

I involved the members of the staff in the decision-making process. This is not my show, I told them. This is OUR show.

It's not up to me, it's up to all of us to make this work. Even down to those on the line staff, I insisted they understand: "You have to buy in. You must be committed." I won't say this trust I placed in the members of the staff, particularly the hold-overs, was always rewarded, but at least I gave them the opportunity to excel at their jobs. Even some of the new ones I brought did not always live up to my expectations.

My overall approach worked, and we began to make great strides as a team. People began to get excited and motivated, partly because of my excitement and motivation. I told them we were looking forward to the days WHEN we became an accredited community mental health center, not IF we received accreditation. I informed them of the possible consequences if we failed to meet the guidelines for achieving this distinction.

I told them, and I somehow got them to believe, that we could be as good as any community mental health center in the state, or in the country, for that matter. I told them we could rise above past problems and overcome our old reputation.

A realization that we had turned the corner, a vindication for all our efforts, came with accreditation. I took over as CEO in November 1995. By July 1, 1997, formal accreditation was conferred upon the center.

It was a heady moment, a reward for a lot of very hard work on the part of all the employees.

But we weren't done. This was no time to rest on our laurels. What we wanted was for the people in the community and the people in the industry to look upon us as the best provider of services and the best employer it was possible for us to be.

Being the best, we decided, was the least we could ask of ourselves, and the least our clients and community could expect of us.

To make certain this commitment became known outside of our own little world, I began meeting with key people in the community. These included officials in local and regional government, especially the juvenile court judge and key child welfare services leaders. I developed good working relationships with these people. I let them know I was fully aware of past problems, but that these were in the past. I admitted up front that we were far from perfect, and that we were probably going to stumble a time or two on the road to major improvements. But, I went on, we were trying for perfection, as impossible as that was to achieve. Our intention, I strongly asserted, was to provide the best service possible.

I encouraged others on my management team to go out into the community and do that same thing. You need to show your faces, I said to my staff, to the people from whom we are seeking client referrals. If they are having problems, you need to both know about them and to deal with them.

From the beginning, I had always attempted to keep an eye on the public image of the center. I had sought to develop good public relations practices, and to get good "reviews" in the local paper.

I wanted to make certain that our name was in front of people.

A lot of folks simply didn't know we were there. Unfortunately, for many of those who were aware of our existence, we were the last place to which they wanted to turn for either help or employment.

It is not easy to turn that kind of public attitude around.

Once we received our formal accreditation, it became obvious to those with whom we had been having these discussions that we were not joking around.

We weren't all lip service.

Gary Community Mental Health Center was truly moving forward.

Power Point 6:

■ ■ ■ ■ ■ ■ ■ ■ ■ ■ ■ ■ ■

Life Rewards Action. Personal success requires planning and then acting to carry out your plan. To have a plan without taking action on it is like having an automobile with no fuel. Purposeful action results in accomplishment. When the task is satisfactorily completed you will know the joy and satisfaction of personal achievement.

CHAPTER SEVEN

The Name Game

❧

Wake up. The hour has come to be more responsible. Change this world by starting with yourself. The world is not going to change until you change.

— Dr. Betty Shabazz

During my tenure at the Gary Community Mental Health Center, the reputation of the place has been greatly improved.

The name has also undergone a dramatic change, as well.

For quite some time after I took over as chief executive officer of GCMHC in November 1995, I felt that one of the ways of enhancing our image in the eyes of the public and officials might be to rename the operation altogether. There were so many negatives connected with Gary Community Mental Health: the long waiting lists, the in-fighting among board members, the frustration among employees, a reputation for delivering poor services when they finally did get delivered, the stigma associated with the term "mental health center."

As parents and grandparents often tell us, a bad reputation is one of the most difficult things to overcome. In some ways, it is true that we never get a second chance to make that first impression. For many people, both clients and members of the community, the first impression of GCMHC was less than an impressive one.

Some members of the board of directors also suggested the idea of rechristening the operation, and I began to give the matter more and more serious thought.

While the facility is located in Gary, Indiana, and we are deeply committed to serving the needs of the city and its residents, we also felt it was important to make it known that we wished to provide services to the broader community, to not only the entire county but also to citizens living across the nearby state line in Illinois.

One of the ways to accomplish this, I felt, was to change the name to something that would better reflect our commitment to serve a broader territory.

In keeping with my policy of including staff members in decisions made about their place of employment, I asked for recommendations on possible new names for the center. I only received a handful of suggestions, and the best of them was from a man on the staff, Rod Johnson.

Rod came up with "Edgewater." He later told me he got it from a community in the Chicago area.

I liked it right away.

Gary sits right on Lake Michigan. This naturally means that seemingly everything in and around the city has the word "lake" in its name. "Lake" this and "Lake" that abounds.

In seeking a new identity for the city's community mental health center, I wanted to avoid the commonplace, and anything with "lake" in it definitely fell into that category.

"Edgewater," I felt, accomplished the same thing, indicating our proximity to the Great Lake, but different enough to be appealing.

As a new title for the center, Edgewater was not universally embraced, either by the employees or those in the community. But there was enough support for it that I was comfortable making the switch.

However, renaming a community institution of any kind is not as simple as that.

"Edgewater" was only part of the equation. What should the rest of the name be?

We played with a lot of different possibilities. Some gained serious consideration, such as "Edgewater Community Services," while others were tossed aside rather quickly.

I felt strongly that the new name should signify for us a kind of rebirth, the dawning of a new day. I wanted it to be a testimony to the fact that we were moving ahead, and putting our old baggage far behind us.

One of the things we wanted to stress was that the center offered a comprehensive array of services to our clients and our community. We didn't want to be thought of as just the place where troubled juvenile offenders received counseling or just the place where those with substance addictions could turn to for help.

Those of us on the inside of the organization knew that we were much more than those individual services that the public perceived. What we offered was an entire system of care, with a number of different levels depending on the needs of the client.

The new name thus evolved to "Edgewater Systems."

But, no, I said. That sounds a little bit like a water company of some sort.

The motto of the Gary Community Mental Health Center had included the phrase "helping people to balance their lives." It's difficult to improve upon that as a mission statement.

The new name, signifying a new start, was finally born:

"Edgewater Systems for Balanced Living."

The name change became official in April 1998. I personally thought at first that it was a little long as a title, but it has worked out well.

We conducted a public relations campaign leading up to and following up on the announcement of the name change. I did some local radio spots and wrote about the switch in a column I had begun doing for the local paper.

As of August 2000, Edgewater Systems for Balanced Living has an annual budget of close to $13 million. We have roughly 250 employees.

All of these achievements did not come about solely as a result of my efforts, by any means. I wish to emphasize the great amount of cooperation among many, many people, both inside the organization and out, that was required to bring about a new community institution to meet the new challenges placed upon us.

Services have expanded greatly in the years since I became president and chief executive officer. A methadone maintenance facility has been added. We have completed construction of a brand new fifteen-unit apartment building for semi-independent clients. We've started an emergency shelter for young people that is almost always full.

In all, five to six new programs were added during my first five years as head of the center. The only program we dropped was our in-patient services, because it was simply not cost effective and other operations in the area could provide that kind of care.

Edgewater Systems for Balanced Living is a significant entity in Gary and the surrounding community. Any major urban area needs, and needs badly, a community mental health center, one that is strong and viable.

Not everyone can afford private mental health care and often those who can least afford it need it the most. Community mental health centers exist to fill that need.

We help to improve the quality of life for all the people who need our services, especially families and children.

Edgewater Systems for Balanced Living is a resource for our community, and a much-needed one.

Power Point 7:

■ ■ ■ ■ ■ ■ ■ ■ ■ ■ ■ ■ ■

Know that change is inevitable. It will always occur. When change happens, it can be uncomfortable and even disruptive. Change can be scary. So much so, that you may find yourself being resistive to change. This may happen subconsciously, even though you know the change may be for your own good. When you resist, you sabotage your own chances for personal growth and awareness. To resist change is futile. It will happen whether you want it to or not. Therefore, you need to develop the wisdom and courage to identify and take advantage of the opportunities that are created when change happens. Accept it willingly, openly, and with flexibility. Open your mind to new challenges and new possibilities.

CHAPTER EIGHT

Going the Distance

❧

If I made it, it's half because I was game enough to take a lot of punishment along the way and half because there were a lot of people who cared enough to help.

– Althea Gibson

I ached all over.

Every bone in my body hurt. Every muscle.

Everything.

I vowed: "Never again."

I was not suffering from some sort of massive hangover. I've seen the ravages of alcohol, and want no part of it, thank you.

No, I had brought this misery upon myself in a completely different way.

I had decided to get in better shape, and this was one of the eventual results.

Save for a lucky few, most of us eventually realize, as we begin to get older, that caring for our bodies is a more involved and complicated task than it once was. We become more "high-maintenance."

When I was in my early thirties I decided to take up running. This grew out of a realization that I needed to engage in some form of exercise in order to stay healthy, although my main motivation was to keep my weight where I wanted it to be. Running, I felt, was a good way to do that. It also had the added benefits of being inexpensive and convenient.

Running for me started at a local high school track in Gary, Indiana. It also involved creating time in my busy schedule, but I knew that getting and keeping myself in better physical shape would enable me to maintain my busy schedule. I began by running a lap on the track and then walking a lap. Once I was comfortable with that, I would run two laps and walk one. I gradually built up my distance in this way until I was running four laps around the track, which is one mile.

I stayed at that level for quite a while, and might have been content with that amount of activity, but then I happened to meet an avid runner. John introduced me to running as not merely an activity but also a sport, and I began to see in it the kind of challenge to which I had consistently risen throughout my life. My new friend took me to some five-kilometer races in which he ran, but at first I was only a spectator.

It had never entered my mind that I could run as far as three miles. Also, the idea of running as fun was completely foreign to me. I recalled how in junior high gym class that running was used as a punishment. Our instructor would force us to run around the track as a penalty for misbehavior, and I hated it.

While attending these races with my friend, I became acquainted with several members of the Calumet Region Striders, a running club in the area. Both these people and my friend would joke with me before the events started.

"You going to get in a race?" they would ask.

"No," was my simple answer.

"You can do it," they would encourage me.

"Never," I said. "Nope. No way. Not going to do it."

My friend the runner kept urging me to go a little further each time we ran together. His gentle cajoling eventually worked, and after a time I was running not my one mile but a dozen circuits of the track at a time, three miles.

Also around this time, I made friends with another runner who helped encourage my development in the sport. Earl Smith was the football coach at Lew Wallace High School, where I had started my exercise program. He later became a member of my board of directors at Edgewater Systems for Balanced Living.

Earl motivated me to stick with my running program, meeting me at the school track at 5:30 every weekday morning, and only a little later on the weekends.

Before long, I entered my first race. I certainly didn't win, by any means, but I finished.

I discovered with me a capacity for taking delight in the resultant feeling of accomplishment.

My running friends were not done with me. Now that you've done five kilometers, just over three miles, you can run a ten-kilometer race. Once again I resisted. I felt that 3.1 miles was the plateau at which I would be content to stay. Once again, they didn't take no for an answer. I caved in to that mild peer pressure and ran a six-mile race.

Guess what? I made it through, and I didn't die in the process.

I began to consistently run in ten-kilometer events and longer. I began to feel better going that distance and my times in the races improved. I'm the kind of person who generally takes challenges to the next level, even when I have decided against it. The next level for me as a runner was to participate in a half marathon. That is the truly daunting distance of 13.2 miles. Two of my friends from the Calumet Region Striders, Rich and Jerry, convinced me to take this next step, and offered to assist me in training for it.

They mapped out a course and even ran it with me. I didn't do too badly in the practice and so I entered and completed a half marathon in Calumet City.

You can probably see what's coming. That's right. No sooner had I completed that half marathon than my friends began working on me to move up to an even higher level of difficulty and achievement.

"If you can do a half marathon," they said, "you definitely can run a marathon."

That's over twenty-six miles!

"No way," I told them.

They said: "Way."

And they were right. Rich and Jerry, who had mapped out the half-marathon course for me, came up with one that was twenty two miles, close enough for marathon training. It was the exact distance between one friend's house in Gary and the other's in Wheaton, Indiana. That first time out we maintained a fairly sedate pace. We stopped a good deal. We drank plenty of water. It went well.

They had me convinced.

You see, there was a time when I was a teenage single mother that I thought I would never get a high school diploma, but now I had two master's degrees. There was a time when I didn't think I'd ever amount to much beyond flipping burgers or doing some other low-paying, menial type of work, but now I was rapidly rising in the field of management and personnel for nursing homes and community mental health centers.

There was a time when three miles seemed like a major milestone for me as a runner, but now I had already gone twenty two miles.

Two weeks later I participated in the 1992 edition of the Chicago Marathon. My two running mentors started out with me, but soon left me in their dust. Well past the half-way point, at about the seventeen-mile marker, I was forced to stop and take some water. Up to that point, I had consumed water while I kept moving. I walked for a time after stopping and then picked up the pace again. At mile twenty three or twenty four, I caught up with Rich. The distance was taking a toll on him, as well. We talked one another through those last two or three miles, providing the kind of encouragement that helps us all achieve our maximum, to go beyond what we might think is our limit.

A few feet from the finish line, my friend resumed a faster pace and completed the race ahead of me.

Men.

I was about wiped out when I crossed the finish line myself. But I had completed a marathon. My time was four hours, twenty seven minutes, nothing to brag about but nothing to be ashamed of, either.

By the time I got home, I was in absolute agony. I was sore everywhere, particularly in one hip. I soaked in a hot bath for the longest time and then went to bed until well into the next day.

When I finally rose, I said to myself: "I am never doing this again."

I sincerely meant it. I was glad to have run the race. There was a tremendous feeling of accomplishment at having achieved the milestone of completing a marathon, but I was never going to do that to myself again.

Guess what?

I've now run a total of six marathons. After the Chicago Marathon in 1992 I took some time off from running, but found that I missed it. Once my sore hip was better, I resumed running with my friends from the Calumet Region Striders. By 1994 I was feeling good enough, or I had sufficiently forgotten how badly I had felt, to try running again in the Chicago Marathon.

I have completed marathons in Columbus, Ohio; Washington, D.C.; and Honolulu, in addition to Chicago. My best personal time is four hours and seventeen minutes, but that's fine with me.

I now run between five and seven miles a day, five or six days of the week. When training for an upcoming race, I also run about ten miles a day, or more, on weekends.

I have gained some new running partners over time, and one is especially faithful and never misses a morning with me. Her name is Corrie and she is my Airedale.

For me, competing in marathons is about being able to set that as a goal and achieve it. It's also, and perhaps just as importantly, about not disappointing my friends and fellow runners. They encourage me and motivate me to do my best as a runner, and I respond to that. I also do the same for them.

To me, it's all part of the living process, the process of learning as we go through the years, of being open to new things and of gathering lessons from those around us.

I will be running more marathons in the years to come and even have plans for putting together a marathon training team at Edgewater Systems for Balanced Living, where I am the president and chief executive officer. I see this as a way of getting others at my place of work to get themselves into better shape as well as a means of raising funds to support the center's programs.

After all, I started out going once around a track.

Power Point 8:

■ ■ ■ ■ ■ ■ ■ ■ ■ ■ ■ ■ ■

Always be willing to take it to the next level.
Continually challenge yourself. Empower yourself
with a confident, positive attitude. In so doing, you
will find a never-ending desire to accomplish much
more, to achieve greatness, and to stand above the
crowd.

CHAPTER NINE

All Dolled Up

❧

Our lives are either spent in doing nothing at all, or in doing nothing to the purpose, or in doing nothing that we ought to do. We are always complaining that our days are few, and acting as though there would be no end to them.

— Seneca

Matter, the physics books tell us, can neither be created nor destroyed.

Time is a bit more flexible, not to mention vulnerable. Time can be wasted. It can be killed. People do time and bide their time. They fritter it away. For many of us, there is never enough time.

I like to look at time as something that is out there to be discovered, like another continent to the ancients or a distant planet for astronomers.

I think that we can FIND time, to do the things that we must, and that we should also FIND time, to do the things that we want to do. In our increasingly busy world, I realize time is not an easy quantity to come by, but I think it is almost a necessity to find a little to do the things that our hearts tell us we should do.

Along with running to keep in shape, one of my favorite pursuits involves dolls. I both collect and make dolls. I find the time to devote to these activities because it is something I enjoy, something special to me.

The earliest figures recognized as dolls date back to around 2000 B.C. Play dolls made of wood fabric were found in the tombs of the ancient Egyptians. Dolls were produced for the children of ancient Greece and Rome, between 100 and 800 A.D.

In the Middle Ages, from about 800 to 1600 A.D., dolls were made of such humble materials as baked clay, wood, linen and wool. For the next three hundred or so years, the privileged nobility of Europe enjoyed the luxury of fashion dolls of all sizes. These dolls traveled all over Europe, and some even crossed the Atlantic to the American Colonies.

It was in around 1870 that the great French tradition of porcelain doll making began.

Seeking to compete with the French, German firms began creating porcelain dolls between 1880 and 1930 that were more affordable.

The most important development in the doll world in recent times is the emergence of dolls crafted for discriminating adult collectors.

When I was a little girl, a doll was at the top of my Christmas wish list every year. Some Christmases went by and no doll appeared under the tree for little Danita.

Then, as now, something new and different in the world of dolls seemed to come out just before the holidays, a new model or line of dolls that would fill me with longing. Santa wasn't always able to answer my wishes. I remember one year that Davida, a girl who lived down the street, received a Barbie doll with three or four different wigs. No matter how much I craved one of my own, however, it was not to be.

As I grew older, dolls became somewhat less important to me, although I never completely lost my love for them.

As an adult, working in my third job, my first in the field of community mental health, I met a man whose wife was a member of a doll club. The man, who handled insurance for the mental health center where I was in charge of personnel, spoke frequently and eloquently about his wife's collection of dolls. Although I never got to see the collection, his remarks piqued my interest in dolls once again.

Not long after that, my eye happened to stray across one of those ads in magazines for collectible items from the Franklin Mint. This one was for a doll, an exceptionally beautiful and appealing one. By that point in my life, I did not have to wait on Santa Claus or Christmas or anything else. Acting on an impulse that felt pretty good to fulfill, I obtained the first doll for my collection. It is a lovely little baby wearing a christening gown.

Doll one led quickly to doll two, this one of a Gibson Girl, the likeness of a young American woman in the 1890s as depicted by artist Charles Dana Gibson.

At that point, I had given up any aspects of the "party life" in order to be able to concentrate on my studies while I was in college. By the time I was embarked on a career I felt a need for an outlet above and beyond just work. In spite of having to care for my children and pay attention to my job, I felt it was important to have a well-balanced life that included some hobby or interest outside of these important parts of my world.

I think all people should have this, something really and truly their own.

It involves finding time, of course, but it can be done.

The next addition to my collection was another baby. This was my first doll of color, the first of many. Not all of them are African-American dolls. I have dolls depicting peoples from the world over. Dolls of color are not easy to find, and the ranks of people collecting such dolls are growing, in large part due to their relative rarity. The works of those few artists who are producing dolls of color are much in demand.

The shift from mere collecting to making came about as a result of another hobby I took up. I enrolled in a class in ceramics, initially crafting little accent pieces to place around my house or to give to friends and family members as gifts. It wasn't easy arranging my schedule so I could attend the classes, but it was something I dearly enjoyed.

What I said to myself was: "That's my time to do with as I will."

From my experiences in ceramics class, I began to see the possibilities for making my very own dolls. I approached the instructor about this and got both encouragement and some advice.

The first doll I ever made was as a gift for the tenth birthday of my youngest daughter, Kyla. It was a special experience, not only because I had fun doing it and it turned out well with the help of my instructor, but also because it was going to be a present for my daughter that she just might have for the rest of her life.

Of course, when I gave the ceramic creation to her I had to explain this wasn't the kind of doll that can be played with and should be kept as a fond memory. As it turns out, the doll eventually wound up in my collection.

For me and many collectors and creators of dolls, porcelain dolls are the ultimate. Those French were on to something back in the 1870s. Porcelain dolls are the prettiest dolls, I feel, and they are so very fragile and delicate. In my collection are dolls made from all kinds of material: wood and vinyl and plastic and ceramics, and I love them all.

But I love my porcelain dolls the best.

My switch from making ceramic dolls to crafting porcelain ones came about as a result of a feature story in the local newspaper.

It was about an older area couple who had their own "doll hospital." They did repairs on dolls, many so old that they had belonged to the grandmothers and great-grandmothers of local residents. In addition to fixing damaged porcelain dolls, the husband-and-wife team also taught classes in doll making.

It wasn't long after I read the item in the paper before I paid the couple a visit. I asked them lots of questions, as I generally do, and learned about the doll-making process. I thought to myself, "Hey, I can do this." I soon suited actions to thought and in short order had made several porcelain dolls of my own.

It is not a simple process, and many steps are involved. One starts with either commercial or self-made molds for the faces and limbs of the dolls, and sometimes the body as well. The material, called "slip," is poured into the molds after which it is permitted to set. Once this takes place, the molds are carefully removed and the still-wet face and arms are allowed to dry. They are then cleaned of rough edges after which they are fired in a kiln. The painstaking job of painting these sections of the doll begins, and between each painting there is another firing in a kiln.

A doll might require anywhere from three to five applications of paint, with up to a dozen hours spent in the kiln after each one.

The material is exceedingly delicate and there is a risk of the parts cracking or breaking at each step in the process. I've broken many pieces, and it is really a terrible feeling, almost disheartening, to have this happen just as the creation is about to be finished.

But when everything works just right and the finished product is assembled, the costume picked out, the eyes put in place and the wig attached just right, it is a work of art. There is a tremendous feeling of accomplishment to turning out a work of art.

After getting my start with the "doll hospital" couple, I found another instructor who taught me more advanced techniques for creating porcelain dolls.

My new instructor has her own business, Hello Dollies, located in Frankfurt, Illinois, about forty miles from my home in Gary. Nancy Kerner, who owns Hello Dollies, is a grand master in doll making and has received several different certifications in the craft from the Doll Artisans Guild. Her specialty is reproductions of very ancient dolls. She is very dedicated to authenticity, an expert on the history of antique dolls and a stickler for details.

She wants the work of her students to be as close as it possibly can be to the antique doll being reproduced.

I have been going to Hello Dollies since the early 1990s, and I learn something new on almost every visit.

My doll collection, which began with the little baby doll from the Franklin Mint, has now grown to about two hundred. I have made about 60 percent of them.

It is difficult for me to pick out a favorite from among the dolls in my collection. It changes from time to time.

Time.

In my household, the time I dedicate to collect and making dolls is called "Danita time." Occasionally my husband and I will get into a discussion about our schedules, who can get to what errand. Once or twice he has pointed out what all I might be able to accomplish if I weren't going to doll class. I smile sweetly and say, "I'm going to doll class."

You can make the time for the things you want to do, the things that are important to you. Doll making and collecting is a priority of mine because it provides relaxation and respite for me. I can afford this somewhat expensive hobby and I can devote the time to it because I deserve to be able to do so. I have worked hard in order to be able to set aside this time for myself. It's my fun time, and this time well spent.

Power Point 9:

■ ■ ■ ■ ■ ■ ■ ■ ■ ■ ■ ■ ■

Find out what makes you happy, then go for it. We are often so busy in our worlds of ceaseless activity, that we seldom take time for the things we enjoy. Slow down! Take time to ensure that you have a good healthy balance between work, family, and play. This will give you peace of mind and your life will be much less stressful.

CHAPTER TEN

City in Distress

❧

All the darkness in the world can't put out the light of the one candle.

— Confucius

Gary, Indiana, in 1969 was a thriving city.

Flames from the steel mills, Gary's industrial heart, were visible for miles around. Jobs, good-paying ones, were available for seemingly all who wanted them. Local businesses prospered.

Then the bottom fell out.

The flames died down, and they have never burned as brightly since.

The steel industry in 1906 created what was once nicknamed "The Magic City" out of uninhabited Lake Michigan waterfront.

A downturn in the fortunes of big steel made the magic go away.

In a two-year period, following that economic high point in 1969, Gary went from thriving to throttled. During that time span, 20,000 of the city's 27,000 steelworkers lost their jobs, and lost them for good. Like their fathers and grandfathers before them, these were mostly men who had gone into the mills straight out of high school. They expected the work to see them into retirement, as it had their fathers and their grandfathers.

Suddenly, all that was gone, and gone forever.

Practically overnight, an entire way of life for a community and its residents had vanished, gone up like a puff of smoke from a stack. People faced uncertain futures. Dreams died, and died hard.

Roderick Johnson, a case manager for Edgewater Systems for Balanced Living, Gary's community mental health center, remembers what life was like before times turned bad. He knew of a time when someone could walk out of high school one day and into U.S. Steel the next, and make top dollar. The money the steelworkers made spread throughout the community.

"Everybody had a job, money was rolling in, downtown was flourishing," Johnson recalls. "The town was flush with money."

Gary was also a "one-industry town," according to Frankie McCullough, former board member of Edgewater Systems' predecessor, the Gary Community Mental Health Center. When that one industry went belly-up, Gary had nothing to fall back on.

A lot of people left in search of greener pastures. Those who stayed behind were hoping against hope for an economic turnaround. They faced the kinds of stress that can lead easily to depression, which caused some to turn to alcohol or drugs.

Richard Hatcher was Gary's mayor during this devastating period in the history of the city. He recalls presiding over a city at a time when not only were 20,000 people being put out of work, but also a well-meaning government program was turning people with mental health problems out of institutions and onto the streets. As if Gary's mental health picture wasn't already bleak enough, with the problems that can result from a ruined local economy, the community found itself faced with many people who had severe mental illness.

In the early to mid-1970s, a federal program was created to help towns in the Rust Belt and other parts of the country that were facing a losing battle against foreign imports. It was called "Model Cities," and one outgrowth of the program was the availability of funding for community mental health centers.

Model Cities ushered in the existence of Gary Community Mental Health Center. The Carter Administration was in power by the time the center was ready to be dedicated, and First Lady Rosalynn Carter herself was on hand for the ceremony.

Gary, Indiana, was and in many ways still is a city in distress. This, of course, leads to families in distress.

What began as the Gary Community Mental Health Center, and which has now evolved into Edgewater Systems for Balanced Living, offers counseling and therapy to help distressed people get back on their feet. I know. I'm the president and CEO of Edgewater Systems. The folks who work with me listen to people's problems and help provide them with new directions for their lives, or a means of being more content with the lives they lead.

One of the ways in which we do this is very simple. We tell those who turn to us for help: "You're not alone, and what has happened to you is in no way your fault."

As an organization, Edgewater is committed to providing a positive and nurturing environment for families and children to help them not only be able to exist in this community, but also to be able to thrive.

By the time Edgewater Systems celebrated its 25th anniversary in 1999, over 15,000 children and more than 50,000 adults had received treatment through the center and its programs. We offer a wide range of programs for people of all ages and in all circumstances of life. We are especially attentive to the mental health needs of local children, offering services that range from outpatient treatment to residential facilities to emergency shelter.

Programs offered at Edgewater Systems provide judges in the local criminal justice system with a viable alternative to incarceration for first-time and more minor offenders.

Every year, millions of people fall prey to emotional problems. Others run afoul of drug and alcohol abuse, whether directly as users or through watching it happen to friends and loved ones. Many of those with emotional or addiction problems go undiagnosed, and even more go untreated.

I am proud to say that the presence of Edgewater Systems for Balanced Living reduces the chances of that happening to residents of Gary and surrounding communities. We work tirelessly to provide treatment to those in need and, almost as importantly, offer education and awareness programs to help prevent people from one day requiring counseling and therapy.

We can't reignite the flames of the city's steel mills, but we can rekindle hope in the hearts of its residents.

Power Point 10:

■ ■ ■ ■ ■ ■ ■ ■ ■ ■ ■ ■ ■

Have a "Plan B." Most of us spend a tremendous amount of time worrying about things we have no control over. Often decisions are made or things happen that affect us, but we have no direct input or influence over those decisions or actions. No problem! Have a fall back plan. Always remember that anything can happen, and if it can, it often will. Always know that you control your own destiny. Be prepared for the worse. But know that it is only a bump in the road on the way to greatness.

CHAPTER ELEVEN

Cases in Point

All of you reading these words have loved someone, have done someone a kindness, have healed a wound, have taken on a challenge, have created something beautiful, and have enjoyed breathing the air of existence. Every moment you make a difference.

— Random Acts of Kindness

Arnita suffered from clinical depression for nearly two decades.

The former mental health center client never sought help for this at-times debilitating condition until the late 1980s. She didn't seek help for a very simple reason: She had no frame of reference for knowing anything was wrong with her. In spite of her depression, Arnita landed a high-pressure job with a railroad. The stresses from work didn't help her condition.

Arnita finally sought help after becoming disoriented while attempting to visit the home of a friend. It was a place she had been to often, but Arnita was finally forced to stop at a pay phone and ask her friend to come and get her. The friend advised her to get help.

Arnita did. She is one of the many success stories for community mental health, and when our center celebrated its 25th anniversary in 1999, Arnita was kind enough to consent to appear in a video making that milestone.

She had this to say:

"People don't necessarily know what's wrong with them when they're going through it. It's very important to have someone to turn to and to find out that you're not the only one out there, either, suffering from it."

No, Arnita, you are not alone.

Others also consented to be in our anniversary video because when they really and truly needed help, Edgewater Systems for Balanced Living was there for them. Among these was Terry, who received assistance at our drug treatment facility, which we call The Turning Point. It was a turning point for Terry, and she badly needed one.

At the time the video was made, Terry was 38 years old. She had been using drugs since she was 12. For much of her adult life, Terry was a heroin addict. With remarkable candor, she speaks of having once loved heroin, having loved the drug even more than she loved her own children.

From time to time, Terry would clean up her act and get herself free of drugs, but she kept sliding back into that life. During the slide that preceded her stop at The Turning Point, Terry became HIV-positive as a result of sharing needles.

"I don't deserve to die," Terry says plaintively in the video. "I'm a human being, just like the next person."

When Terry turned to The Turning Point, she was treated like a human being. She speaks with wonder of encountering drug counselors who actually cared for and about her. At other drug treatment facilities, Terry recalls being given her maintenance medicine and being shown the door. Things were different at The Turning Point, where she also received some compassion and some individual attention.

It made a difference.

As Terry says in her concluding remarks on the tape:

"I'm happy today. I have a life and a reason to live, and no one can take that away from me."

At Edgewater we provide help for people seemingly beyond help. Some additional examples:

• When she was admitted to one of our programs as a 16-year-old, "Maxine" brought a lot of troubles with her. She also brought lots of troubles to those around her.

Maxine, not her real name, was diagnosed as having an "adjustment disorder." She was referred to Edgewater as a result of sexually inappropriate behavior, including sexual promiscuity, in school and at home and in the community. A victim of exceptionally poor self-esteem, Maxine was seeking acceptance, both at home and from her peers, by any means necessary. When she failed miserably at this as a result of her negative behavior, she eventually withdrew from those around her.

In addition to all this emotional baggage, Maxine also suffered from cystic fibrosis.

This is a congenital disease of children that is character-ized by a malfunctioning of the pancreas along with frequent respiratory infections. As a result of her cystic fibrosis, Maxine was often hospitalized.

Put it all together, the emotional problems, the unac-ceptable behavior and the terrible disease, and Maxine was in a world of hurt when she turned to us at Edgewater.

During the course of her treatment at the center, Maxine learned to accept her illness. We also helped her to explore resources outside of the center and beyond her family situ-ation. She registered for programs through the Indiana Division of Disability, Aging and Rehabilitative Services.

When she arrived in October of 1998, Maxine had little going for her.

In June of 2000, she received her high school diploma. She has once again become active in the community and has begun to participate in dance classes.

Maxine, a girl once nearly helpless and practically hope-less, went to the senior dance and attended her senior prom.

She danced, beautifully, at both.

• The referral came from the Lake County Office of Fam-ily and Children Services.

We'll call the subject of that referral, a young, unwed mother, "Ms. B." Office of Family and Children Services caseworkers had been forced to remove Ms. B's two young children from her because she had shown herself to be incapable of providing them with a stable living environment. It was suspected that she badly neglected the children.

Ms. B stayed "here and there," in her own words, after her children were placed with relatives. Ms. B began receiving treatment for her mental health issues, and for a time it appeared she might stand a good chance of having her children returned to her custody. But she soon fell back into her old ways, and the opportunity passed her by.

Ms. B was out of treatment for a while, but eventually returned for services at Edgewater. With the help of our counselors, she began the difficult task of putting her life back together. Edgewater's Family and Youth therapists and case managers also provided emotional support to the children during this difficult period.

Ms. B participated in psychotherapy, and responded to the treatment very positively. With the assistance of case managers, she was able to apply for housing and school. After finding a nice place to live, Ms. B made enough progress in her psychotherapy that she was able to have overnight visits with the children. Those experiments worked out well.

After a while it became apparent to our counselors that Ms. B had a stable living situation and, far more importantly, had achieved emotional stability as well. This was a gratifying moment for the many people at Edgewater who had worked so hard with the young woman to get her to see light at the end of the tunnel.

After several court reviews over a period of eighteen months, Ms. B was awarded full custody once again of her children. Following a brief period of monitoring and maintenance by Edgewater personnel, her case was closed.

We last heard that she is working regularly and that both of the children are in school and actively involved in church and at a local community center.

- By far the most heart-wrenching situations that we deal with at Edgewater Systems for Balanced Living involve children who have suffered abuse, whether it is mental or physical abuse.

Maryann Kannappan, a therapist in the Placement Diversion Program at Edgewater, discusses one such case in her contribution to our anniversary video. Maryann works with children who are at risk of being removed from their homes, either as a result of their own behavior problems or because of some situation involving the parents or guardians. In either case, Maryann relates, these tend to be very troubled youngsters.

Few though, are as troubled as the 5-year-old boy Ms. Kannappan was treating at the time the video was made.

The child had been diagnosed as suffering from major depression with psychotic features. He had made attempts to take his own life, which, as Maryann points out, is quite rare in someone that young.

The boy's condition was a direct result of the severe abuse he had suffered practically from birth. His mother was a child herself, only 14 at the time she gave birth. She was totally unprepared to be a parent. She actively disliked her only offspring, perhaps resenting the loss of freedom he represented for her. When he was but an infant, and a slap with an open hand would be severe punishment and constitute child abuse, this boy's mother frequently slugged him with her fists, Maryann recounts.

"She told him at an early age that she hated him," Ms. Kannappan says.

The result of all this was a child remarkably fragile emotionally. Because he was completely unable to talk about the feelings raging around inside his small body, the boy frequently acted out.

Boy, did he act out.

As Ms. Kannappan relates in the video, there were times when the boy's acting out was so severe he had to be restrained. In one instance, she says, an attendant as big as a football player had great difficulty in handling the boy.

At such times, Maryann says, the little boy would feel as if he was fighting for his very life.

In trying to bring some peace to this child's troubled mind, Maryann Kannappan turned to something all children should know a lot about, but which he did not, and that was play. She would play with him, and as he came to accept her as a playmate, Maryann would provide narration of his activities that permitted him to see this play as an outlet for the feelings bottled up painfully inside him.

Through play, he found an outlet for his inner turmoil.

There are many, many cases where the people at Edgewater have made a major difference in the lives of those with terrible troubles. These were just a few examples.

Power Point 11:

■ ■ ■ ■ ■ ■ ■ ■ ■ ■ ■ ■ ■ ■ ■

Remember that there is always someone out there who is worse off than you are. In the big scheme of things, your own problems are minor. Others have experienced much worse. Reach out to others who are in distress. Such acts of human kindness become self-reinforcing because they answer a deep-seated need to connect with others and allows you to see your own worth and importance.

CHAPTER TWELVE

Being There

It is one of the most beautiful compensations of life that no man can sincerely try to help another without helping himself.

– Ralph Waldo Emerson

I suppose I could find a pretty good job in virtually any kind of business or industry.

Over the years, I have acquired management skills that would stand me in good stead in many fields of endeavor. I could almost assuredly find positions within private industry that pay a great deal more than I earn as president and chief executive officer of a community mental health center in Gary, Indiana.

But I have no real desire to seek out better-paying, more prestigious employment at this time.

I derive a great deal of satisfaction from being where I am and doing what I do.

For one thing, it means a great deal to me to preside over an organization that brings so much help to the troubled people of my hometown. I did not have an easy time of it growing up, but the Gary that I first knew as a child was a prosperous place. The massive layoffs in the steel industry in the late 1960s and early 1970s hit Gary especially hard, and in many ways the city has never fully recovered from the blow.

The counselors and therapists at Edgewater Systems for Balanced Living, and the Gary Community Mental Health Center before it, seek to cushion the blow. It's not easy. An entire way of life went by the boards for practically the entire population. The emotional pain that kind of dislocation causes people is difficult to calculate, but evidence of it is all around in Gary.

The quality of life that people are able to enjoy in Gary today is greatly improved, I think, by the existence of Edgewater. If it were not for a community mental health center, very few of those in need of mental health services could afford them.

When people live in a highly urbanized environment, particularly in a dense inner city, many of this country's social ills become all too apparent: drug abuse, alcoholism, depression, stress-related illnesses, behavior problems among children, domestic violence, child abuse. The list goes on. Sadly on. These are things people experience all across the country, and in all kinds of settings, but they seem both worse and more readily apparent in an inner city.

Couple that with the lack of jobs, good jobs, that continues to afflict Gary and you have a population badly in need of the types of services offered by a community mental health center.

Lots of the people who turn to us are hopeless. They see no alternatives. They feel they have no options. Life has dealt them a lousy hand of cards and they have no choice but to play with them.

They are wrong, and it is a wonderful feeling to be part of something that leads people to realize that.

One of the things I like best about what I do is that I and many of my coworkers at Edgewater have experienced or have had those close to us experience exactly the kinds of things many of our clients are going through. It makes me feel so good that what I and the others at the center do contributes to the ability of people to lead better lives, to take the steps necessary to change their lives for the better. We are often able to dispense the precious commodity of hope, and there are few things more rewarding.

The most heart-wrenching cases we deal with involve children, and these are also the most important assignments we take on. Children are so very vulnerable, so much more so than adults.

Whenever an opportunity presents itself to the staff of Edgewater to make a difference in the life of a troubled child, we make this our highest priority. Achieving success in this area is among the most rewarding aspects of service in the field of community mental health. Working at Edgewater, our counselors often get the opportunity to rescue children from difficult situations, even when those situations are a result of their own destructive behavior. A lot of these young people simply need somebody to listen to them, somebody to show some concern.

When we can do this, and we get many opportunities to do so, it warms my heart.

Sometimes it seems so many more children find themselves in terrible emotional situations these days. I think this is due, at least to some extent, with our society getting better at identifying and reporting problems that involve children.

While the residents of Gary and the area surrounding the city are especially in need of the services offered by a community mental health center, economic privation is not a requirement for such services. Community mental health centers are needed practically everywhere. Even when times are good, some people feel bad. They have problems, issues. Some people simply cannot deal with the facts of everyday existence. They are unable, for example, to get over the death of a loved one. Or they find themselves incapable of handling the stress involved with seemingly simple jobs.

Even when the economy in this country is good, drug abuse is taking place, people are falling prey to alcoholism, children are being abused, husbands and wives are fighting.

It is no simple task to maintain a really good, productive and dedicated staff at a place like Edgewater, and this is for a number of reasons. First and foremost, community mental health is not a very high-paying industry. Second, many of those attracted to the field want only the fun aspects involved in improving mental health. They grow weary of the more demanding, but less emotionally rewarding, aspects of the profession. Just like any other job, being a counselor involves many different responsibilities, including a great deal more paperwork than some people bargained for when they began their training. It is not the kind of job where people walk in, listen to some problems, dispense a little advice and then head home. That's only a part of what the employees of a mental health center do.

Most of the people who work at Edgewater Systems really want to be there. They realize they will never get rich, but they find their rewards in other aspects of the work. There are those who come on board and then fail to rise to the challenge. They move on, usually on their own but sometimes with a little help.

Maintaining the quality of care the people in our community deserve is about setting standards, creating expectations, establishing a "culture" within the organization as to how we view and treat people who come in for service.

I have two hopes that I hold onto, two hopes that help sustain me as I go about my work running Edgewater Systems.

One of them is that one day the stigma attached to mental health problems will be a thing of the past. I know this will not be happening anytime soon. A lot of work remains to be done to get more and more people to understand that those who succumb to the pressures of everyday life are really no different from those who appear to be coping better.

Some day, I firmly believe, those who need a bit of help from counselors or therapists or psychologists or psychiatrists won't be ashamed of having done so. That goal is, perhaps, a long way off, but I have dedicated myself to bringing it about.

Mental health truly and simply involves how we view life, and how we respond to its challenges. To that extent, we all have our own mental health issues.

My other sincere hope is that eventually the true worth of what those in the community mental health field do will be adequately recognized and compensated. I am a firm believer that this, too, will one day come about.

To help bring improved funding about, I and my

organization are involved in the advocacy work done by a number of trade associations. Each year, the Indiana Council of Community Mental Health Centers, of which Edgewater Systems is a member, puts forth a legislative agenda for our state lawmakers. On the national level, we back the advocacy efforts of both a countrywide trade association for mental health centers and the Child Welfare League of America, both of which also annually develop positions and measures for which we seek Congressional backing.

On a local, state and national level, I personally do as much advocacy work as I can to improve funding for mental health, not only from governments but also from foundations and other private organizations. I do this because we need increased funding not merely to better reward those in the field, but also to attract more people to mental health down the road.

That's because the numbers of those in need of our services aren't getting any smaller as the years go by. They just keep getting bigger.

And yet, funding for mental health programs tend to be among the first cut when government officials perceive a need to scale back spending. It often seems as if we are never very high on the list of priorities when it comes to spending, that other voices cry out about their needs louder than we are able to cry out about ours, and this frequently with unfortunate results.

For example, I am constantly amazed at how quickly government officials are willing to cut off funding for drug treatment programs. Those same politicians will find themselves voting, just as quickly if not more so, for increased funding to prosecute and incarcerate the very people those eliminated drug treatment programs could have helped.

For young people thinking about a possible career in the area of community mental health, I offer encouragement of several different kinds.

First, as I have mentioned, I think greater notice of and appreciation for the work done by mental health professionals is only a matter of time. With that will come better financial rewards for those doing the work.

There is also, though, a degree of satisfaction and gratification to be found in the community mental health field that does not exist in many other areas. Being able to change, and change for the better, the lives of troubled people is probably one of the most rewarding things a person can do.

At Edgewater, many of my employees come from the community that they serve. They often find themselves treating as clients people with whom they went to school and the relatives of friends. They are often able to help these members of their own community get back on their feet and get back to leading their lives.

That to me is a wonderful thing.

There is another side benefit to being involved in the mental health field, and that is the way in which it helps practitioners to grow and develop as individuals. Those of us in the profession tend to become much more knowledgeable than most folks about human nature, and to have a better understanding of not only different people but also ourselves.

Most of us tend to develop improved awareness and relationship skills, both within ourselves and toward others.

This, too, is wonderful, in my opinion.

Power Point 12:

■ ■ ■ ■ ■ ■ ■ ■ ■ ■ ■ ■ ■ ■

You help yourself when you invest in others. There is nothing more emotionally satisfying than when we give much and expect little in return. Having the willingness to help other people and to put their needs and desires before your own is reflected in the attitude and actions of an emotionally secure person. An emotionally secure person practices and teaches understanding, tolerance, and service to others.

CHAPTER THIRTEEN

Crime Time

❧

*Law and equity are two things which God hath joined
together, but man has put asunder.*

– Charles Colton

Quick: What's the fastest growing industry in the
United States?

That's the kind of thing most people would like to know.
They would want a tip on the area of the economy that is
growing the fastest of all. They would like to get some stock
in that particular industry.

Well, we all have stock in the industry. Every citizen of the
United States is an investor, but none of us are getting rich.

In fact, as a nation, we are being impoverished by this
industry in many different ways.

That's because the fastest growing industry in this country is the prison system.

And that is a shame.

Let me once again state my dismay at how ready, willing
and able politicians in this country are to cut funding for

drug treatment and other programs that divert people from taking the wrong path in life. Those same politicians are just as ready, just as willing, just as able, if not more so, to vote millions toward the construction of new jails and prisons. Many of our political leaders trumpet their tough stance on crime and point to these monuments to society's failures as proof they are doing what needs to be done.

Get the criminals off the streets, they assert, and crime goes away.

This is shortsighted beyond belief, and shamefully wasteful. On the one hand, there is no comparison between the costs related to treating people for the problems that are leading them toward time in prison versus the costs of keeping someone behind bars. I say this without any fear of contradiction because for years I have been involved with developing and delivering treatment programs in as cost effective a manner as possible.

Permit me to use an automotive analogy: Regular oil changes and proper maintenance, while a drain on the household budget, can keep a car running for years and years. Failure to do so can ruin the engine, and replacing it will cost many times more than all the oil changes that were skipped.

It is my understanding that during the 1990s more than 800,000 prison and jail cells were added to what was already in existence when the decade dawned.

But spending far more money than we have to represents only the tip of the iceberg when it comes to what outrages me about this country's policies toward those deemed to be offenders of society.

The financial impact is a factor, although statistics relating to the relative expense of treatment and diversion programs as opposed to incarceration costs are not easy to come by.

The real impact of policies that put people in prison who don't need to be there is on families, and especially children. This impact is felt the hardest in the African-American community.

In this country, more and more people are being incarcerated every day. The prison population in the United States has more than doubled in the past decade.

So-called "get-tough-on-crime" programs are partly to blame, as are laws that establish mandatory sentencing guidelines.

In this, the new millennium, the statistics relating to the prison population are shameful.

I read recently that one of every one hundred thirty men in the United States is in prison.

Currently, almost one of every three African-American males under the age of 30 is under the control of the country's criminal justice system.

They are either in prison, on probation or on parole.

The percentage of this country's men involved with the criminal justice system is nothing in which we can take any pride, and it is a long-standing issue that's just getting worse.

An equally dramatic but far more recent development regarding prison population growth deals with women. Women are being incarcerated at a higher rate than at any other time in the nation's history.

The number of women in the prison system has tripled over the past decade. Tripled. On any given day, there are well over 100,000 women behind bars, either in jails or penitentiaries or prisons. The majority of these women are sub-stance abusers, and their criminal activity can be directly linked to their addictions.

For both men and women, longer terms behind bars are becoming the norm in this day and age. Due to stricter sentencing requirements, many federal and state prisoners are serving terms that are over 54 percent longer than the terms they would have gotten for the same offenses ten years earlier.

Mandatory sentencing, please forgive the expression, "sucks."

Plain speaking is the only way to adequately express my disgust with this trend, which prevents judges from using the wisdom and experience gained behind the bench in determining what is and is not an appropriate sentence for a given individual. Policies that hamstring judges in terms of using their judgment on a case-by-case basis simply perpetuate the problems they are meant to address.

Take mandatory sentencing for people convicted of drug-related crimes. Getting most of those who are arrested for drug crimes off the streets does not get the drugs off the streets.

If anything, the level of drug activity in inner city areas sometimes seems to go up at the same time there are crackdowns on so-called street pushers. Such crackdowns never seem to reach the real drug kingpins, the ones involved in the importing end of things. Instead, only the messengers are arrested and locked up, while the bigger fish remain free to recruit replacements with promises of ready cash, and lots of it.

Locking up the little people in the drug world does not solve the problem of drugs on the street, and instead just creates a host of other problems.

Drug arrests have nearly tripled since 1980, to more than 1.6 million today, according to Justice Department figures. Further, the harsher sentencing laws have contributed to increased numbers of these offenders being imprisoned. These measures, which prevent the sentencing judges from considering the convicted person as an individual, have increased by four and a half times an individual's likelihood of receiving prison time for a first conviction.

The average length of time served in a federal prison for conviction on a drug offense back in 1986 was just under two years; 22 months, to be exact.

A mere four years later, following the adoption of mandatory sentences, the expected length of time a person convicted of the very same offense could expect to serve had tripled to 66 months.

It should come as no surprise that the current drug policy in the United States has been a dismal failure. In fact, it would be fair to say that we are losing what is often referred to as the war on drugs.

National policies that place a greater emphasis on punishment over prevention and treatment are not working, and they have had a disproportionate impact on low-income communities and minorities.

Three major areas of the government's policies aimed at battling the spread of drugs in our society have led to the dramatic increase of incarceration for African-Americans for drug offenses. These are:

1) the concentration of drug law enforcement in inner city areas;

2) the harsher sentencing policies, particularly for crack co-
   caine; and,

3) looking first to enforcing laws rather than paying much,
   if any, attention to such potentially worthwhile activities
   as prevention and treatment.

Millions of poor children have become "drug war or-
phans" while their parents serve lengthy jail terms.

The numbers connected with the prison population are
just that to most politicians: numbers.

The painful truth is that each of those numbers represents an individual, and the vast majority of those individuals
have families. Many, many of them have children.

The damage done to families, particularly African-American families, is just as important as the financial burden and,
in my mind, even more so.

When a parent goes to jail or prison and leaves behind
children in the outside world, it's a pretty safe bet those children are going to be left in less than ideal circumstances. Such
children often receive no proper guidance. They have greatly
reduced chances of growing into healthy, mature adults.

These children end up in broken families, in single-par-
ent households, and more often than not in poverty.

Despite the enormous wealth of this country, in spite of
the economic boom of the 1990s, fueled largely by the stock
market, the rate of child poverty in the United States is among
the highest of all industrialized nations.

It is one thing to, as a society, give up on an adult who
has made some bad decisions in life. It is quite another to

visit those bad decisions on his or her children, and to sentence those children to grow up poor.

Unfortunately, children living in poverty are much more likely than those who start off life in better circumstances to suffer from problems relating to physical health, emotional well-being, readiness for school, achievement in class and, down the road, employability as adults.

It is difficult to determine exactly how many children are affected by the incarceration of their parents. As more and more people end up behind bars for longer and longer periods of time, greater numbers of children are left behind to suffer the emotional consequences.

According to the Child Welfare League of America, the most widely accepted estimates, and they are only estimates, indicate that the approximately 100,000 women and 1.23 million men in prison are the parents of around 1.53 minor children. An estimated two thirds of the women doing time have children under the age of 18.

While I have indicated my disdain for lawmakers who opt for the easy and seemingly popular solution of prisons over prevention and treatment, the media is hardly blameless in all this. The mass media has a tendency to portray drug use and other social ills in such a way that people feel they will be safer only when those involved in drug abuse and crime are off the streets.

The way the media portrays people involved in drug crimes has a great deal to do with our perceptions of who belongs in prison and why.

Stereotyping is involved, and this is no more helpful to individuals and their individual problems than blanket sentencing requirements. There is little or no attempt by the national media to look at the underlying issues involved in inner city drug abuse and crime in general.

The variables that lead people to be standing in front of judges awaiting sentencing are extraordinarily complex. The problems involved do not lend themselves to easy solutions.

I do know one thing, and I know it from my experiences at work every day.

What I know is this: treatment can work and does work. Once a person has made up his or her mind, for whatever reason, either by themselves internally or as a result of a little help from the courts, treatment can be very successful.

Lives can be changed, and not only for the individuals receiving treatment, but also for their friends and family members, their employers and co-workers.

We do it daily at Edgewater Systems for Balanced Living.

I don't want to give the impression that treatment for drug abusers or others who have turned to a life of crime is in any way an easy or simple matter. Far from it, both from the perspective of the individual in treatment and the counselors. Any time you talk about making changes, it's scary. It just is.

Often the people we see at Edgewater who have developed drug problems know no other way of life. It's what they have seen around them from the time they were children, and no one comfortably abandons the only type of existence they have ever known, even if they are aware in their hearts that it is wrong and self-destructive.

Even people with absolutely no emotional problems are resistant to change. How comfortably do we adjust to finding a different way to get to work when construction closes down the route we have taken for years? We tend to make ourselves comfortable with the way we are leading our lives, and change is almost always accompanied by some form of discomfort.

For those caught up in drug abuse, change is even harder. More often than not, drugs are merely a crutch to help overcome other problems in their lives. Abuse of drugs and alcohol becomes a tool for not having to face reality.

A high percentage of those who receive drug treatment at Edgewater Systems have exceptionally low self-esteem. They have no confidence that they can make it through life, through any given day, without the assistance of drugs. They aren't capable of realizing that from the very beginning, and increasingly over time, drug use merely added to their inability to cope with life.

Other issues, from a lack of worthwhile adult role models to child abuse to perceived limited opportunities, confront most people who turn to drugs as the easy way out.

These issues must be gotten through before the process of recovery can begin.

The way to get through those issues and began that recovery process is treatment and counseling, the kind offered by community mental health centers and other professionals. This is where and this is how people with drug problems and other problems that lead them to commit crimes can find help.

This is where and this is how people can begin the process of becoming productive members of society and the parents children need in order to grow up in the same mold.

People with problems need to have their voices heard.

They do not need to hear the slamming of cell doors.

Power Point 13:

■ ■ ■ ■ ■ ■ ■ ■ ■ ■ ■ ■ ■

Apathy has no place in the world of emotionally healthy and personally successful people. Resolve to make your community and the world a better place and to ease the suffering of others. Find an issue that you care deeply about. Actively work to find a solution. Your efforts can make a world of difference in the lives of those who have little or no hope.

CHAPTER FOURTEEN

Leading the Way

❧

We are not merely here to make a living. We are here to enrich the world with a finer spirit of hope and achievement—and we impoverish ourselves if we forget the errand.

– Woodrow Wilson

The term "leadership" conjures up different things to different people; after all, we are all our own dictionary, each providing slightly different definitions for words based on life experiences.

In Webster's, leadership is defined simply as "the ability to lead."

"Bartlett's Familiar Quotations" contains the following:

"Leadership and learning are indispensable to each other." This was to have been said by President John F. Kennedy, but he never got the opportunity to do so. The quotation is contained in remarks prepared for delivery at the Trade Mart in Dallas on Nov. 22, 1963, the day Kennedy was assassinated.

Historian, educator and public official Arthur M. Schlesinger Jr., in his 1965 book "A Thousand Days," wrote:

"Above all he (President Kennedy) gave the world for an imperishable moment the vision of a leader who greatly understood the terror and the hope, the diversity and the possibility of life on this planet and who made people look beyond nation and race to the future of humanity."

In the inspiring book "The 21 Indispensable Qualities of a Leader: Becoming the Person Others Will Want to Follow," America's foremost expert on leadership, Dr. John C. Maxwell, wrote:

"What separates leadership theorists from successful leaders who lead effectively in the real world? The answer lies in the character qualities of the individual person."

I have given a great deal of thought to leadership and have read extensively on the subject. When I turn my mind to the issue of what makes a good and effective leader, I think about a person who has the ability to sway the attitude and the opinions and even the actions of others. Just about anybody has the ability to be a leader, although not everybody bothers to try.

Using my own personal definition of leadership, it is clear that we all have the ability to influence others, from those around us every day to people we meet for the very first time. I believe leadership is a skill, and one that can be developed over time. As is the case with so many skills that take time to acquire, learning to be a leader takes practice and requires work. Hard work. Leadership also involves a trial and error process. Error is a part of it. Mistakes will be made. To take no risk of being wrong is to seize no opportunity to be right.

Leaders must be willing to make mistakes, and then to learn from those mistakes.

While Dr. Maxwell wrote of 21 qualities of leadership in his 1999 book, I define the aspects of leadership in a third of that number. I call my personal views on the subject "The Seven C's of Being a Good Leader."

Those qualities are:

1) **Character.** This, to me, refers to the moral, ethical and emotional qualities that distinguish an individual, and the ability to personify these qualities in both word and deed. We are all of us frequently confronted with difficult, even adverse conditions and situations. Handling crises, whether at home or at work or in other aspects of our lives, does not necessarily help develop character. Making decisions about handling these situations does reveal our character. As John Maxwell wrote, "We have no control over a lot of things in life. We don't get to choose our parents. We don't select the location or circumstances of our birth and upbringing. We don't get to pick our talents or IQ. But we do choose our character."

I did not choose a father who was a very negative influence on me in my early life. I did not choose a mother who showed weakness when I needed her to be strong. I did not choose to be born and reared in a poor part of Gary, Indiana. But I have been able to choose how I lead my life and what I do with it.

2) **Courage.** To me, this aspect of leadership involves caring about principles, not perceptions. Naturally, most of us care about people having a favorable impression of us.

It takes no special courage to cultivate the good will of those around us. A leader, however, is someone willing to stand up for his or her convictions, no matter how it will be viewed by the rest of the world. A leader must be willing to take risks in this regard.

All of us must make many choices in our lives, big and small, momentary and long-term. The test of leadership comes when those choices involve showing integrity or giving in to compromise. The individual who chooses not to compromise on a matter of principle, who stands up for what he or she believes, and does so regardless of the odds stacked against them, to me that person is showing a lot of courage.

3) Commitment. Obstacles crop up in our lives on a daily basis. Oppositions arises. Barriers are thrown up. A true leader shows the commitment to keep forging ahead in spite of obstacles, opposition and barriers.

A true leader will adhere to his or her strongly held convictions, regardless of how the rest of the world feels about these convictions.

A leader has both the will and the strength to continue struggling, to keep on getting back up no matter how many times he or she gets knocked down.

4) Cautious attentiveness. Good leadership requires more than just character, courage and commitment. As essential as those factors are, they can be wasted if a leader acts without taking the time to gather information, and making certain as much as possible that the information is accurate.

Effective leaders seek to obtain all the facts before making a decision.

This, obviously, is not always possible, but once as many facts as can be obtained are gathered, the good leader then considers the options, looks at the alternatives and considers the consequences of different courses of action.

Intuition does play a role in leadership. Gut instinct is very definitely a factor. But the leader who acts without information is failing to do his or her best to ensure that the actions will be successful.

5) **Connectability**. Without a talent for building good relationships, leaders make their decisions and determine the courses of action in a void. Which is to say, they do virtually no leading at all. Remember, I said leadership involves the ability to sway the attitudes, opinions and actions of others. The "connectability" aspect of effective leading involves the ability to understand and work with others, which is the only way in which a person can have an influence over others.

Building good relationships is how we can acquire power, and I don't mean to use the term in any negative sense. Power, in this instance, is practically the same thing as leadership, in that it can involve the ability to inspire others to get things accomplished. Particularly as personal power involves getting others to work toward a common goal, it can be a definite positive. To get disparate people on the same page, all sharing the same vision, requires power. It is something that we receive, not something that can be taken, and this involves establishing a relationship with those around us.

In order to have good working relationships, and thus exert influence over others, there must be an element of trust. They must trust you, personally, and trust that what you are trying to influence them to do is the right thing to do, that it is for the common good, whether in the workplace or for society in general.

6) Contribution to the welfare of others. Leadership should involve service to others. How often, throughout our lives, do we run across people who help us in ways big and small? Probably, almost assuredly, a great deal more often than we realize. A good leader seeks to give back that which he or she has received in the way of assistance.

It is important, essential, really, that this giving back be genuine, that it comes from the heart. Leaders are able to put the needs of others before their own desires.

As an example, I serve on the board of directors of the Gary Public Library. I know why I am there: I want to help the library be successful, to move forward, to benefit the community. I know how much the presence of libraries has helped me in my life. I know the worth to a community of a good library system.

Some people who serve on volunteer boards are there for very different reasons from my own. They serve on these boards as a means of obtaining prestige, of enhancing their appearance within the community. Their "service" is a lot more about what it provides them, rather than what they can provide for the community.

To me, that makes a tremendous difference, not only in the reasons the service is being offered but also in the quality of that service.

7) **Creative perception**. Worthwhile leaders have a vision. They are able to think beyond just today, to consider much more than just current circumstances. This aspect of leadership is not merely about planning, but is more about dreaming. Instead of worrying and thinking, "What if...?" Creative perception on the part of a leader entails, "What can be?"

Dreaming of what the future can hold provides the spark to the planning and goal-setting that is at the core of making dreams become reality.

Leadership is exercised at different levels, and I feel we can and should expect different things from leaders at these various levels.

NATIONAL

Nationally, I do not believe we can expect any leader, no matter how powerful, to solve all of the problems that confront us as citizens of the country and of the world. But, and this holds true for leaders at virtually any level, what we can expect of our national figures is that they have the common good in mind. I want my national leaders to ask themselves, "How can I help the most people? What can I do that will provide the greatest benefit to the greatest number of individuals?"

On a national level, we need people who are passionate about their values and beliefs, because only those with a true passion can keep from being swayed by the myriad influences that are brought to bear on them by various competing interests. A good, solid value system serves to help a president, a congressional figure, even a federal bureaucrat stay on course. By a good and solid value system I mean knowing and understanding what is best for the greatest number of people.

STATE

Coming a little closer to home, I get a favorable impression from those seeking to lead at the state level when they genuinely seek to understand the needs of their constituents. I get the most favorable impression when they try to do this on as individual a basis as possible. Certainly I realize that it's impossible for a state representative or other state government official to know what's what in the back yard of each and every person they are seeking to serve, but some proof that the individual has done his or her homework is important.

To use my own example, when I am dealing with an elected state official or a representative of some state agency who has bothered to become informed about the issues facing community mental health or public education, my confidence level in the decisions that individual makes goes up significantly. Whether it's introducing new legislation or interpreting existing rules and regulations, the state official who is informed about the specific factors relating to the affected industry is much more likely to do the right thing.

It all comes down to the "cautious attentiveness" aspect of leadership I described earlier.

On the other hand, I get more than mildly annoyed with state officials who are trying to promote their own personal agenda, and doing so without bothering to become informed about the individuals, organizations and industries their decisions will have an impact upon. Some come into appointed or elective office with their own ax to grind and they don't let the facts get in their way.

Personal prejudices and preferences must be put aside by those working in public service and on the public payroll.

COMMUNITY

Although I am involved in professional organizations that operate on both the national and state level, it is at the community level that I, and all of us, can exert the most influence. The trick is to exert this influence for the common good.

For me, as chief executive officer of a human service provider, showing leadership involves looking at the best ways in which to coordinate the resources within a community. The next step is figuring out the ways in which these coordinated resources can improve the quality of life for our citizens.

Within the human service sector, this isn't always easy, and that's where leadership very definitely comes into play. At the community level especially, we must be able to set aside "turf wars" and determine how we can all come together to make decisions that allocate resources so that the most people can derive the greatest benefit.

FAMILIES

The numbers of people involved get considerably smaller once we begin discussing leadership at the family level, but in fact the individual responsibility to exercise authority wisely increases dramatically.

Leadership at the family level involves both positional and personal power. By positional power, I refer to the nominal head of household, someone who, based on their position within a family, has control over the others. Whether it is the father or the mother, this is generally the individual who is perceived externally as being the leader of the family.

There is also such a thing as personal power within the family structure. This goes back to the "connectability" factor of being an effective leader. Personal power in a family involves the ability to make emotional connections with the various members of the family and exert influence over them. Personal power frequently has little or nothing to do with the individual's position within the family. After all, when there's a baby in the home, the question of who is really in charge is an easy one to answer.

Regardless of the type of power, and therefore leadership, a member of a family has, it is the duty of that individual to help the entire unit reach its fullest potential.

This never stops, as long as more than one member of a family remains alive. It is as true of the children as it is of the mother and father.

All of us continue to grow throughout our lives, or at least we should, and a family that is full of love and care for one another can be the greatest of tools for facilitating that growth.

INTERNALLY

Leadership within one's self involves having the willingness and the ability to take charge of our lives, and to exercise control as much as possible over how we use time.

This internal leadership involves recognizing that we all need to take the time to rejuvenate ourselves, to rekindle our spirits and our minds so that we remain in balance mentally, physically and spiritually. This does not involve withdrawing, at least not often and not for long, from those around us, our friends and family and coworkers. It does entail self-examination.

All of us need to have balance in our lives, and sometimes the only way to achieve that balance is to take the time out to consider how best to obtain it. For me, this involves pursuing my main hobbies of running and the collecting and making of dolls.

Sometimes the most valuable part of a given week or day is the time we take to be by ourselves, to sit back and reflect on where we are with our lives and where we are going. It is important, practically invaluable, to analyze the situation in which we find ourselves and determine a course of action.

Without exercising some leadership from within, what happens to us is not a product of thought and planning.

We owe some care about taking the next steps in our lives to not only ourselves but also to the rest of the world.

Power Point 14:

■ ■ ■ ■ ■ ■ ■ ■ ■ ■ ■ ■ ■

Commit yourself to make a difference in your world. Look for opportunities to do good by others. Leave a positive impression on everything and everyone you touch.

CHAPTER FIFTEEN

At the Heart of It All

❧

My family keeps me centered. They tell me when I need to turn the dial down.

– Earl G. Graves

With apologies to Charles Dickens, family is the best of influences and the worst of influences.

Family is at the heart of it all.

It is within the family that we are shaped. It is from the family that we derive our value system. Our first role models are almost always from the family. Our first experiences of dealing with other people almost always involve the members of our family. The strongest ties, the connections that will last a lifetime, are forged within a family. Character, to a tremendous extent, is shaped by family.

The best of families nurture us.

The worst do not.

It is up to all of us as individuals to work to keep families strong. We must reaffirm the essential role family plays in our stability and survival. It is even more incumbent upon those of us in the human services field to make sure families have the resources available to them that make success and achievement possible. The importance of this cannot be stressed enough. Just as families have the strongest influence to help children grow and reach their potential, so also do they have the strongest influence for holding children back, for producing people incapable of getting along in society.

Right now, I do not think the family as an institution is doing all that well. In fact, I believe far too many families are in trouble. The reasons are all around us, and include record numbers of children living in poverty and record numbers of fathers and mothers being imprisoned. Drugs and racism only add to the obstacles that stand in the way of families helping children to succeed.

Many of our national policies, including those aimed at reducing a supposed dependence upon social welfare, have not served to strengthen families. In fact, quite the opposite is often the result.

So far, we as a nation have not found effective ways of addressing the problems that beset our families. I will be among the first to admit that I do not have all the answers. The issues are so diverse, the problems so very complicated.

I do know that dealing with these issues, solving these problems, requires a holistic view of our society. Too often, politicians act to address one perceived difficulty without first looking to see what impact it might have elsewhere. Before more effective strategies can be found to help put more resources at the disposal of families, our leaders must look at the problems that beset society as a whole, not in a piecemeal fashion.

Let's take drug abuse as a brief example. Yes, it is true that many people who get involved in drug trafficking do so because of the money that is involved. But, no, that is not the only reason. Too many of the people caught up in this lifestyle are there because they had no hope; they felt there were no other options. None. Without hope, people will cling to whatever presents itself. As a nation, we can do better than permitting a segment of the population to cling to the desperate hope that being involved in the drug trade is a way out of grinding poverty.

Beyond the external conditions that pose problems for families in the United States, there are internal factors, as well. Poor communication is at the very top of this list.

Avenues of communication must always be open within a family. Each member of a family has to feel as if they can discuss anything with the others, bring up any subject or issue that is bothering him or her, bring up questions and concerns, and that their voice will be heard. Even the smaller voices in the family, children, need to be heard. We must take the time to listen to the littlest of us.

In fact, effective communication involves encouraging the voicing of issues, asking questions, raising concerns.

Perhaps the most important thing that can be done within the family, and can be done by each of us, is to show love. People, especially children, have a very basic need to feel protected and to feel loved. That sounds so very simple, and it is, but in my line of work I see case after case where people, far too often children, do not feel protected and most assuredly do not feel loved.

Sometimes, you just have to tell the folks around you that you love them.

Tell your brother. Tell your father. Tell your sister or your mother or your husband or your wife.

Be heard.

Power Point 15:

■ ■ ■ ■ ■ ■ ■ ■ ■ ■ ■ ■ ■

Families are forever. They are the lifeblood of a culture and a society. Love your family members unconditionally. Regularly assess the state of your family and always look for ways to strengthen and preserve it by infusing the right values. The futures of your children and your children's children depend on it.

CHAPTER SIXTEEN

Aspiring to Inspire

❦

Some people change jobs, spouses, and friends—but never think of changing themselves.

– Paula Giddings

Motivational speakers.

Inspirational speakers.

The terms are used almost interchangeably, but to me there is a subtle difference that separates one from the other. Motivation, to my way of thinking, is something that comes from within. Inspiration is what we can get from others.

Easily the most famous of the hundreds of people making a living from inspirational speaking is Zig Ziglar. According to the web site for his enterprise, Ziglar has traveled over five million miles since 1970 "delivering life improvement messages, cultivating the energy of change."

Ziglar, whose corporation is based in Dallas, has shared the platform with such distinguished Americans as Presidents Gerald Ford, Ronald Reagan and George Bush, Dr. Robert Schuller, Dr. Norman Vincent Peale, General H. Norman Schwarzkopf and General Colin Powell.

There are many others roaming the United States these days, with different approaches and styles. I believe the majority of them can and do perform an important function in society.

I would love to join their ranks.

I feel motivated to be an inspirational speaker.

I aspire to inspire, although I don't generally derive all that much inspiration from the Zig Ziglars in this world as I develop and hone my own personal message to help people to motivate themselves to make the best of their lives. I do listen to and enjoy some motivational speakers.

In seeking to make myself a better person, and along the way improve myself as an inspirational speaker, I do nearly as much reading as I do listening. I devour inspirational and motivational books of all kinds.

I also listen to many, many different speakers, and not necessarily those billed as either the motivational or inspirational type. I am willing to listen to anyone who has a message, a positive message that is designed to help people move forward in their lives and deal with the problems they face. Whether the topic is preventing child abuse or the latest innovations in treating drug addictions, I seek to glean things that can be useful to me in my own presentations and in my own life.

It might sound altruistic, but I attempt at each presentation I attend, whether at a seminar or a professional conference, to find material and information I can use to then go out and help others. I ask myself, "How can I impart what I have just learned to others so that they can begin making improvements in their lives?"

I do consider myself an inspirational speaker, because

whenever an opportunity presents itself to give a talk to any group, I try to leave them with something that can be useful in their everyday existence, something that can help them.

For me, it's a way of life. I try to view nearly everything I do as being helpful in some way to those around me, both in the immediate and in the greater sense. Whether it's at work or serving on some professional association committee, if what I am doing is not helping people, I ask myself, "Then why are you doing it?"

I do not by any means feel that I have "arrived" as an inspirational speaker, or a person, for that matter. I always think there is a lot more that can be done in terms of my professional development, both my speaking and my performance at work. I constantly look for ways to improve, to find a better means of tailoring the lessons I have learned from my life to fit the needs of wider and wider audiences.

One of the ways in which I strive to improve my speaking is through research. Unlike some inspirational speakers, I do not have a set speech that I make to all audiences. Before putting on any kind of public speaking presentation, I take the time to learn as much as I possibly can about the group before which I will be appearing. I may not know the shoe sizes of everyone in the audience or how many children each one has or where they all were born and grew up, but I will know as much as I can glean beforehand about what makes the organization as a whole tick, what their aims and goals are.

I do this primarily by speaking with either the person who recruited me or a member of the audience that is to receive my talk. I ask, point blank, "What do they want to hear?" Then, just like in high school or college, I do my homework. I read magazine articles and books, or portions of books, that pertain to the subject at hand. I just keep researching and practicing my presentation right up to the time I have to deliver it.

Whenever the format permits, I try to allow time for questions. After all, even the best-prepared speaker can't be expected to address everything that's on the mind of everyone in the audience.

If, by chance, I don't know the answer to a particular question, I make certain to look it up so that I will have the information available the next time. I won't get caught on the same question twice without having the right answer, or at least the very best answer I can possibly find.

During presentations, I always try to determine whether or not I am making a connection with my audience. I do this by reading the body language of different members of the group. Usually, I can tell if they are being attentive, and especially I can tell if they are excited by what they are hearing. Someone will nod over in this section of the audience. Someone in another section will echo the gesture. Someone else might start the applause for a point that particularly hits home.

Fidgeting, glancing at wristwatches, whispered conversations.

These are all signs that I am not making the connection with my audience. This is one of the most uncomfortable feelings I have ever experienced. I feel as if I have failed, and I have to be honest and admit that from time to time I have tasted the bitter cup of failing with an audience.

But there are other times, sublime times, when my message and my audience mesh perfectly with one another. This is extremely exciting for the speaker. There is more enthusiasm throughout the entire room. I, as a speaker, become more enthusiastic about my presentation, which creates still more enthusiasm in the audience, which is still more inspiring to me.

Such moments are worth the occasional copper-penny taste of failing to make contact.

Almost regardless of the topic that I am called upon to address or, really, the needs of the audience to which I am speaking certain things hold true and remain of the utmost importance to me.

The primary one is that I am able to tell the people listening to me that, in the vast majority of situations, they can control their lives. They are the ones who control their own destiny.

I believe this implicitly, and am convinced this is a message that is not hammered home to people early enough or frequently enough.

Far too often, people feel they are primarily controlled from without. The people around them, their environment, the place they were born and the parents they were born to are why things are the way they are, and that's just plain shirking responsibility.

Taking responsibility simply requires us to stop playing the "blame game," to stop readily accepting the role of victim. Too many people today, as T.D. Jakes has pointed out, are too quick to start formulating excuses and rationalizations for why things went wrong, why they should not in any way be held accountable for their problems.

Bishop Jakes is the founder and senior pastor of the 17,000-member Potter's House, a multiracial, non-denominational church in the Oak Cliff area of Dallas.

Ducking responsibility leaves those who practice this approach to life utterly powerless when faced with truly difficult times. People who don't practice handling even minor setbacks are completely unprepared when faced with problems of a very real and substantial nature.

People simply have to know, down in their hearts, who they really are. This means, I firmly believe, that people need to renew the spiritual dimension of their life. The spiritual dimension helps you to know and understand your purpose in life. It is your core, your center, your commitment to a value system. It is that part of yourself that drives all of your thoughts, decisions and actions.

I think inspirational speakers can be of tremendous value by helping people to tap into that spiritual dimension. The best of inspirational speakers can assist us in understanding that we all have something to add to this world, and if circumstances are preventing us from doing this, that there are ways of getting around those circumstances.

Every experience, if viewed properly, is a learning experience. Each learning experience presents us with an opportunity to profit from it and use it as a tool to teach others.

It is important to me as an inspirational speaker, to continue to improve as one, because I sincerely believe I have a message. I also know that I have an ability to relate to people on many different levels and from many different walks of life. The poor and the well-to-do, black or white, women or men, experiences I have had enable me to share my message of hope and of taking charge of one's life with all kinds of people.

While I have never been a man, obviously, and, just as

obviously, never been white, I have had such a wide variety of experiences, with still more to come, that I can almost always find some common ground, some meeting of the minds with any audience that I might happen to address.

So many people today are disheartened, for a variety of reasons and sometimes, when you get right down to it, for no reason at all. They don't have very much confidence, in themselves or those around them.

They are just plain unhappy.

If I can provide any little ray of hope to people who find themselves in that situation, if I can lead them to believe in their hearts that they can succeed at what they want to do if they set their minds to it, then I can fulfill what I consider to be one of my main missions here on earth.

I have been desperately poor. I have known despair. I have suffered setbacks personally and professionally.

Through it all, I have managed to maintain a belief in myself, in my worth as a human being and in my ability to overcome whatever confronts me and achieve whatever goals I set for myself.

This is not easy, and I am the first to admit it. Getting where you want to be, achieving whatever goal you have established almost always requires work, hard work and lots of it.

But then something worth achieving is worth working as hard as one possibly can.

My main message is this:

"If you make the commitment, you can make the change."

Power Point 16:

■ ■ ■ ■ ■ ■ ■ ■ ■ ■ ■ ■ ■ ■

Be a constant source of encouragement to others. Reach out to and empower others by sharing your gifts. You may be able to provide them with an opening into a larger world—one with greater possibilities for personal happiness and achievement.

CHAPTER SEVENTEEN

In the End: Faith

❧

I always had only one prayer: "Lord, just crack the door a little bit, and I'll kick it open all the way."

– Shirley Caesar

I am a Christian.

My faith sustains me.

I rely upon it nearly every day of my life.

It is not necessarily popular in this day and age to make such a statement, and to a certain extent, I can understand why. This is because almost as soon as I put down the words, "I am a Christian" and "My faith sustains me," I feel moved to point out that does not mean I am a religious fanatic.

I am constantly amazed at the uses to which some people put the teachings that have provided the spiritual dimension to my life. How they can have listened to the gentle parables I first heard in my youth and have gotten from them a message of intolerance is beyond me.

Too many people, it seems to me, wear their faith on their sleeves. They attempt to exude the attitude of being so very "grounded" in their religious beliefs, that these beliefs seem to be literally all there is to their lives.

Religion, to me, should be about inclusion, not exclusion.

I try hard to let people know I am a Christian, but without being overbearing about it. I seek to set an example for others through my actions. I feel as if I am a good person in large part as a result of my faith in God.

My trust in a higher power enables me to continue to strive to be a good person, and to feel blessed in doing so.

Religion is a part of my life.

I have two things, primarily, to thank for this:

1) My mother

2) Movies

Permit me to explain. The foundations for my Christian beliefs began very, very early in my life. For some reason, my mother insisted that my younger sister and I attend church every Sunday. We were the only members of the family of whom this was required. Not even our mother accompanied us.

Nevertheless, every Sunday she got us up, got us dressed and sent us off to the neighborhood church in Gary, Indiana. We walked there on our own, sometimes on very cold winter mornings, to be embraced by the loving warmth of the congregation inside.

About the movies: I do not mean to imply that my belief in God was inspired by "The Robe" or "Ben Hur" or "Barabbas" or any other Biblical film. Rather, my younger sister, Denise, and I both loved the movies when we were little and Sunday was the one day of the week we were permitted by our mother to go to the local theater.

But only if we went to church first.

So we went.

As I got a little older, I began to grow away from the church, as young people often do. I began to think of our weekly walks down the street as a burden, a form of drudgery. It was not something I wanted to do, but something my mother was forcing me to do. I did not understand the value of the lessons I was receiving in church.

By the time I was a teenager and young adult, I had moved away from the church altogether.

Still, looking back through the charm of time and with the clarity of maturity, I can see now that I did learn some very valuable lessons there among the faithful in my neighborhood church.

I did not fall back on these lessons until I started getting a little older and began to realize there were a lot of challenges out there, that lots of things can happen to us in life.

It can be wonderfully comforting to turn to something bigger than just one's self in coping with these challenges. To be able to draw upon the spiritual base I had developed without really realizing it made me feel less alone when times were hard.

Initially, this return to a spiritual foundation was almost purely internal. I drew on my experiences, on the Bible teachings from that small neighborhood church, for the comfort I needed when I felt so very afflicted.

After a time, I began to feel the need to once again return to a formal church setting as a means of both proclaiming and reaffirming my faith. I once again wanted that "connected" feeling that comes with spending time in religious contemplation with others. I did find connection, to that feeling, that concept of oneness that comes from being part of a church.

My move back into formal religion was aided by a realization that my own children needed to start attending church. After all, whether I liked it or not, it was good for me when I was a child. I began to go to church on Sundays as much for them as for myself. I am certain they felt they were being dragged along to something unpleasant, that they would have much rather remained in bed.

But I know it did them some good. I know they learned some basic values, the kinds of things that remain with one all through life. I think, after a time, they began to recognize the worth of spirituality in their lives.

It is easy when times are good to let the spiritual side slide. As the old saying goes, "There are no atheists in foxholes." When the going gets rough, appealing to a higher power, drawing on one's faith and praying for improvement is important. Beseeching God for a turnaround when all around seems negative is almost natural.

I feel, however, that it is just as critical to maintain a relationship with God, to work to sustain beliefs, when we reach comfortable stages in our lives. We can readily forget the need to look to a higher power when our worldly needs are being met.

On a daily basis, I think it is important to understand how very much we have to be thankful for, and to give this thanks to Him from whom these blessings flow.

I have had some very challenging times in my life. From these I have learned how to avoid mistakes, and how to profit from the mistakes I did make. From the hard times, I have learned how a person can make changes in his or her life for the better.

In large part, I was able to make these changes in my own life as a result of the values I gathered to me when I was a little girl in that small church.

Further, and I hope my life reflects this, I feel I have learned from those hard times and from those church-taught lessons how to use my experiences to make things better for others, to make them feel they have the ability and the capacity to change themselves for the better.

That is what I have tried to do here.

Power Point 17:

■ ■ ■ ■ ■ ■ ■ ■ ■ ■ ■ ■ ■

There is a life of energy, optimism, and creativity waiting to emerge through you. **Let go and let God!**

CHAPTER EIGHTEEN

Determine Your Personal Power Quotient

❧

Take the self-test on the following pages to determine your own level of personal power. Remember, there are a lot of factors that play into your sense of control and power over your own life. Personal power is ever changing. But, it is manageable.

Personal Power Assessment

SELF TEST

Answer the questions below as truthfully and honestly as you can. This is a self-test. No one will see your answers but you. Use this assessment to improve your sense of personal power and thus your degree of satisfaction with your life.

Self Awareness	Always	Most of the time	Some-times	Never
	4	3	2	1
1. Everything I need to know to be happy is inside of me.				
2. I am responsible for my own happiness.				
3. My feelings and emotions provide me with feedback as to how I am inclined to act or respond to different situations.				
4. I accept responsibility for monitoring and controlling my own emotions.				
5. My past has taught me valuable lessons.				
6. I release all guilt about my past.				
7. I control my thoughts and focus my attention on positive matters.				
8. I am happy for others in their good fortune.				
9. I can state my views without getting angry or upset.				
10. I am guided by my personal beliefs and values in everything that I do.				
Column Total				

Interpersonal Relationships	Always	Most of the time	Some-times	Never
	4	3	2	1
1. I feel that I am easy to like.				
2. I develop supportive relationships.				
3. Although I may disagree with another's lifestyle, opinion, or attitude, I seek to understand them rather than pass judgment.				
4. I focus on being a good listener.				
5. I attempt to make sure that I do not deliberately or intentionally harm others by my words or deeds.				
6. I find it easy to tell people I care about them.				
7. I readily and frequently compliment others.				
8. I attract positive caring people into my life.				
9. I avoid negative people and negative relationships.				
10. I practice unconditional forgiveness.				
Column Total				

Job Satisfaction	Always	Most of the time	Some-times	Never
	4	3	2	1
1. I have control over the type of work I do for a living.				
2. My work is satisfying.				
3. My supervisor is supportive.				
4. I like, respect, and trust my supervisor.				
5. I manage and prioritize my workload.				
6. My relationship with my coworkers is cordial.				
7. I am a competent worker.				
8. Those with whom I work respect me.				
9. I offer suggestions to improve my own work as well as the efficiency of the company.				
10. I engage regularly in continuing education opportunities to enhance my skills.				
Column Total				

Mental & Physical Health/Fitness	Always	Most of the time	Some-times	Never
	4	**3**	**2**	**1**
1. I have a complete physical examination at least once a year.				
2. I am in reasonably good health.				
3. I avoid engaging in risky or otherwise unhealthy behaviors such as recreational drug use, driving without a seat belt, etc.				
4. I avoid smoking cigarettes.				
5. I exercise aerobically at least 4 times a week for 30-45 minutes.				
6. I get between 6 and 8 hours of sleep each night.				
7. I actively control my stress and anxiety levels.				
8. I am able to avoid being depressed.				
9. I eat a balanced diet.				
10. I am within the accepted weight range for my gender, body frame, and age.				
Column Total				

Resilience	Always	Most of the time	Some-times	Never
	4	**3**	**2**	**1**
1. I view challenges as opportunities for positive growth and development.				
2. I consistently challenge myself to do better.				
3. I am persistent. I go after what I want.				
4. I am not easily discouraged. I handle setbacks with ease.				
5. I am willing to take risks to realize my dreams.				
6. I do not worry about things over which I have no control.				
7. Life teaches me valuable lessons each day.				
8. I make an earnest attempt not to blame others for my failures or mistakes.				
9. I anticipate success, but I am not afraid of failures.				
10. I accept criticism with grace.				
Column Total				

Family	Always	Most of the time	Some-times	Never
	4	**3**	**2**	**1**
1. My family relationships are close and supportive.				
2. I have a satisfying and intimate relationship with my partner or spouse.				
3. My family is the most important aspect of my life.				
4. I love the members of my family unconditionally.				
5. I treat all of my family members with respect.				
6. I encourage my family members to pursue their dreams.				
7. My family and I enjoy fun time together often.				
8. I guide my family members towards independence.				
9. I am available to members of my family when they need me.				
10. I am observant and aware of my family members difficulties and challenges.				
Column Total				

Service to Others	Always	Most of the time	Some-times	Never
	4	**3**	**2**	**1**
1. Serving others is important to me.				
2. I get great personal satisfaction from helping others.				
3. I am a good mentor to others.				
4. I donate my time, money, and my experiences to help those in need.				
5. I encourage my family and friends to volunteer or otherwise assist charitable and other worthy causes.				
6. I reach out to others who need help.				
7. When I give of myself, I do so willingly and I don't expect anything in return.				
8. In all that I do, I consider first whether it is fair to all concerned.				
9. When making decisions that affect others, I base my actions on what will do the most good for the most people.				
10. I consistently try to build goodwill.				
Column Total				

Spirituality	Always	Most of the time	Some- times	Never
	4	3	2	1
1. Spirituality is an important aspect of my life.				
2. Through my belief in God, I believe I can accomplish anything.				
3. I regularly pray for others.				
4. God loves me for who I am, not for what I do.				
5. I am guided and supported in every aspect of my life.				
6. I am centered in peace, truth, and faith.				
7. I believe that I am abundantly blessed.				
8. I have unique gifts that I willingly share with others.				
9. God is my anchor. I am one with God.				
10. I regularly attend worship services in accordance with my faith.				
Column Total				

Personal Satisfaction	Always	Most of the time	Some- times	Never
	4	3	2	1
1. I feel that I am in control of my life.				
2. I have short- and long-term goals.				
3. I feel comfortable making sacrifices to get what I want.				
4. I have the ability to make powerful choices and I exercise this ability everyday.				
5. I love myself unconditionally.				
6. I am willing to change and grow.				
7. I feel that I am loved and respected by others.				
8. I try not to be jealous of others who have more than me.				
9. I am optimistic about my life.				
10. I am self-reliant in all matters, including money.				
Column Total				
Grand Total of all Columns				

Add the grand total of each of the columns together for your Personal Power Quotient: _____

Key: Personal Power Quotient:

310-360 Optimal This is ideally where you want to be!

240-309 Dynamic If your score is here, you're doing great! A little more effort and your sense of personal power could transform your life.

100-239 Emerging What steps do you need to take to improve your sense of personal power and control over your life?

0-99 Dormant Wake up! You've got lots of work to do. But don't despair. You've got the power!